HEALTHIER
SOUTHERN
COOKING

HEALTHIER
SOUTHERN
COOKING

60 Homestyle Recipes with Better Ingredients and All the Flavor

ERIC AND SHANNA JONES

Creators of Dude That Cookz®

PAGE STREET
PUBLISHING CO.

PAGE STREET
PUBLISHING CO.

First published in 2022 by

Page Street Publishing Co.

27 Congress Street, Suite 1511

Salem, MA 01970

www.pagestreetpublishing.com

Distributed by Macmillan, sales in Canada by The Canadian Manda Group.

26 25 24 23 22   1 2 3 4 5

ISBN-13: 978-1-64567-472-6
ISBN-10: 1-64567-472-X

Library of Congress Control Number: 2021937983

Cover and book design by Meg Baskis for Page Street Publishing Co.
Photography by Amy Scott

Printed and bound in the United States of America

Page Street Publishing protects our planet by donating to nonprofits like The Trustees, which focuses on local land conservation.

DEDICATION

We want to dedicate this book to Beverly Jones, Eric "Dutchy Boy" Jones Sr., Helen Dupree, Pearl "Momma Pearl" Bynum, Herman "Daddy Paul" Bynum and Oliver "Papa" Jones Sr. The stories and memories I cherish most are the foundation for every recipe we create.

CONTENTS

INTRODUCTION

I remember just like it was yesterday—the first time I turned on a stove to make a meal, or what I thought was a meal. At six years old, I was determined to serve a hot breakfast while watching Saturday morning cartoons, and this wasn't going to be my regular weekend cereal routine. Nope. I was going for eggs and toast. To my surprise, it came out great, and I was intrigued by the cooking process, which later led me to make pancakes from scratch. After carefully watching my mother whip up a batch of batter and subsequently preparing my first stack, my love for cooking was born.

I owe a great deal of my culinary prowess to my mother and grandparents. My mother, Beverly Jones (a.k.a. "T-Bev" to everyone else), was a great cook. Her spaghetti and meatball recipe was so famous that family members randomly appeared out of nowhere when the word got out she was making it.

Spending many summer months in south Louisiana meant lots of time with my mother's parents. My grandfather, who we all called Daddy Paul, was a hardworking man. His prized garden was home to sweet watermelons, crunchy cucumbers, oversized sweet potatoes, juicy cantaloupes and huge bunches of collard greens. My grandmother, who we all called Momma Pearl, was an excellent cook too. She could transform anything my grandfather harvested from the garden into a fantastic meal.

When I wasn't sitting on the kitchen counter anticipating what Momma Pearl would cook up next, I was with Grams, my father's mom. Grams was known for her Sunday suppers after church—and trust me, they were a big deal. Buttery cast-iron cornbread, savory red beans and rice and vibrant succotash were all staples in her kitchen. I learned about the versatility of the cast-iron skillet from Grams. She made everything in it. Not only did I learn cooking techniques that I still use to this day, but I also grabbed some secret tips and tricks.

My mother and grandmothers were fantastic cooks, each with unique cooking styles. Through them, I learned the essential ingredient in every meal, which was love. This spirit of love still lives with me today, and that passion allows me to bring joy to others through food. As the great Maya Angelou would say, "I'm just someone who likes cooking and for whom sharing food is a form of expression."

From making the best out of what I had while growing up, to Valentine's Day cook-offs with my wife, to enjoying unique dining experiences around the world, my creativity in cooking continued to expand throughout my life. Cooking became an art form for me, and I started to challenge and channel my inner "chef." However, along with those happier milestones came loss. Losing both parents—who were considered still relatively young—to health problems forced me to reevaluate my overall health and the food I was consuming. I started researching ingredient alternatives as well as organic and clean foods, and I began eliminating certain proteins from my diet. Those dietary changes are the focus of the healthier recipes in this cookbook.

Dude That Cookz, my wife's and my food and recipe blog, was born from those very changes. Like putting quick and easy spins on traditional dishes by replacing certain ingredients with ones that are better for you. And sharing how to eat healthier without sacrificing flavor. My journey has allowed me to showcase how to enjoy southern cuisine in a new light.

In this cookbook, you will find recipes that will help you maintain a healthier lifestyle by making a few tweaks, adjustments, swaps and substitutions. The seven chapters in this book will take you from breakfast to dinner and back.

The first chapter, "Healthier Southern Comforts with All the Flavor," will showcase southern entrées. You'll find drool-worthy favorites and healthier renditions of my mother's and grandmothers' recipes, like my Low-Fat Homestyle Chicken Meatloaf (page 15), which is my lighter spin on a traditional meatloaf, and Momma Pearl's Pot Roast (page 16), which uses less sodium than you would typically find in a meal that size. And, of course, I had to throw in a few Louisiana favorites! You'll get to enjoy more Louisiana-style recipes with fewer calories, less fat and less salt—be sure to try my Low-Fat Creole Fish Étouffée (page 22), Chicken and Chicken Sausage Jambalaya (page 25) and Creole Okra and Tomatoes with Beef Sausage (page 26).

"The Neighborhood Sandwich Shop" is where you'll find my Veggie Muffuletta Sandwiches (page 55), which will make you forget it is meatless. The lean but mean Creole-Spiced Lamb Burgers (page 64) and bite-sized Bison Sliders with Caramelized Onions (page 67) will get you ready for your next gathering. And no one will guess they are eating healthier.

If soups are your thing, you'll want to make your way to "Wholesome Soups to Warm Your Soul." This chapter is filled with delicious soups, stews and bisques that show how easy it is to enjoy a luscious, creamy soup with minimal fat. If you are a lover of mushrooms, you really can't go wrong with the Five-Star Truffled Mushroom Cream Soup (page 82)—it's rated five stars for a reason. And freshly shucked corn takes the Creamy Corn Chowder (page 77) to the next level, adding the perfect amount of natural sweetness without a drop of sugar.

For small bites, appetizers and starters, head to "A Lighter Something to Hold You Over." Fully Loaded Baked Sweet Potato Fries (page 89) and Oxtails and Potato Croquettes with Sage-Butter Sauce (page 86) are just a few ways to kick off a meal in true southern fashion.

Since you cannot have a main dish without sides, "Calling All Sides—with Fewer Calories" is a must-see chapter. Several of my family's recipes show up there in a healthier form. The Red Beans and Rice with Turkey Sausage (page 122) replaces pork sausage with turkey sausage to lighten things up. My mother's Southern Potato Salad (page 112) is so creamy you won't believe it has fewer calories than traditional potato salad. And there's even Sweet Potato Soufflé (page 130), a recipe born from my love of picking sweet potatoes straight from my grandfather's garden. All great and better for you!

"A Healthier Way to Rise and Shine" boasts healthy and tasty breakfast and brunch options, like Cheesy Grits with Sausage and Peppers (page 136) that take me back to the kitchen with Grams. Say goodbye to heavy cream; you'll be amazed at what a little coconut milk can do.

And since my lovely wife grew up baking, she is giving you all the goodies in the dessert chapter. "The Guiltless Sweet Tooth" is a treat for everyone. Here you'll find Healthier Southern Peach Cobbler (page 151), Sour Cream Pound Cake (page 148) and Low-Fat Sweet Potato Cheesecake (page 153)—every recipe will blow you away. And the great part? You don't have to pass on dessert, because ours are all made healthier—with less sugar and fat but without sacrificing the feeling of indulgence that dessert brings.

Our goal for sharing these recipes is to bring readers a new way to enjoy southern cooking that may influence a healthier lifestyle. All recipes in this cookbook have a more nutritious element. They are either low in carbs, sodium, fat or calories. And as frequently as possible, we have incorporated organic, grass-fed and fresh ingredients to enhance each dish's flavors and nutritional value. We recommend buying organic ingredients whenever possible—from fresh produce, to meat and dairy products, to dried herbs. Eating organic foods reduces the number of chemicals in your diet; they are free of any artificial colors, flavors and preservatives; and as a bonus, they are great for the environment due to better farming practices. Organic food is both delicious and beneficial.

Let's turn great, better-for-you ingredients into healthier southern recipes! Are you ready?

Shanna Jones

HEALTHIER SOUTHERN COMFORTS

WITH ALL THE FLAVOR

Growing up, I looked forward to dinner, no matter how my day was going. It made me feel better about almost anything and seemed to invoke a sense of comfort and even joy. There was nothing a hearty meal couldn't fix!

The main dish was the focus of every meal. And sometimes, it was the only thing on the dinner table. Mainly because there were so many folks to feed, and the entrée was the most plentiful. A bottle of Thousand Island dressing for a quick side salad, hot sauce and white rice could turn any meal into one of the best you'd ever tasted. No matter which grandmother owned the feast for a given evening, she always made sure everyone had plenty to eat.

Staying true to my grandmothers' traditions, I've included hearty dishes in this chapter. The Low-Fat Old-Fashioned Chicken and Dumplings (page 19), Seared Halibut with Succotash (page 38) and Chicken and Chicken Sausage Jambalaya (page 25)—all are complete meals on their own. In fact, you'll be able to feed four to six people with any recipe in this chapter. When you make these recipes, you can be sure you'll have a wonderful meal even if you enjoy it solo. I mean, who needs sides anyway? Well, we'll just leave that discussion for a later chapter.

The recipes you'll find in this chapter focus on the main dishes I learned to cook in my grandmothers' kitchens—dishes like Momma Pearl's Pot Roast (page 16), which cooked so slowly in the oven it seemed as though it would never finish, but you knew it was worth the wait. The tender roast would go straight from the oven to the table. Grass-fed beef, low-sodium beef stock and red wine make this recipe better for you and packs it with nutrients.

Then there is the Low-Fat Creole Fish Étouffée (page 22). Although I grew up enjoying a different version of this dish, this perfectly creamy tomato-based stew is vibrant in color and flavor. It's still one of my favorite dishes to make, and the fact that it's low in calories and fat makes it that much better. And I can't forget the Red Snapper and Cheese Polenta with Creole Tomatoes (page 47)—I mean, anything with cheesy grits is sure to be divine, am I right? For a healthier spin, I've made a few tweaks to reduce the fat and swapped out a few traditional heavy ingredients for lighter ones. My family always looked forward to this tried-and-true Creole recipe and hopefully you will too.

When I hear the words "southern hospitality," I think far beyond a warm welcome. I think of comforting dishes that make you sit back in your seat to ready your belly for the next bite. They make you feel good. They are nostalgic dishes you have been eating most of your life. They just feel like home.

The sentimental value these recipes hold for me keep me connected to my roots. And even though I have made some lifestyle changes since my childhood, I still find ways to keep those memories alive. These mains are warm and fulfilling yet showcase a healthier spin on the traditional without missing a beat.

LOW-FAT HOMESTYLE CHICKEN MEATLOAF

2 lb (908 g) lean ground chicken

½ cup (28 g) panko breadcrumbs

⅓ cup (33 g) grated Parmesan cheese

¼ cup (60 ml) canned light coconut milk

1 large egg

1 tbsp (5 g) dried basil

2 tsp (4 g) paprika

1 tsp garlic powder

2 tsp (4 g) black pepper, divided

1½ tsp (3 g) Himalayan pink salt, divided

1 tbsp (9 g) minced garlic

1½ cups (240 g) coarsely chopped onion

2 cups (480 ml) tomato sauce

¼ cup (55 g) light brown sugar

1 tsp Worcestershire sauce

½ tsp onion powder

¼ tsp ground mustard

Who knew chicken meatloaf could be so good? One of the downsides to your typical meatloaf is the amount of fat. Well, this version is healthier, perfectly moist and certainly not lacking in the flavor department.

This meatloaf is prepared in much the same way as beef meatloaf recipes, with a few tweaks. The ground meat is combined with panko breadcrumbs instead of traditional breadcrumbs to retain moisture, coconut milk replaces the heavy cream and Parmesan cheese adds tenderness and flavor. The mild flavor of the ground chicken picks up the flavors of the seasonings and herbs, and the homemade barbecue glaze turns this into a meatloaf masterpiece. You gotta try it with the Creamy Mashed Potatoes (page 125) or Southern Green Beans and Potatoes (page 126)!

Preheat the oven to 375°F (191°C). Lightly grease a 5 x 9–inch (13 x 23–cm) loaf pan or a 9 x 13–inch (23 x 33–cm) baking dish.

In a large bowl, combine the ground chicken, panko breadcrumbs, Parmesan cheese, coconut milk, egg, basil, paprika, garlic powder, 1 teaspoon of the black pepper, 1 teaspoon of the Himalayan pink salt, minced garlic and chopped onion. Mix the ingredients together. If you are using a loaf pan, transfer the meatloaf mixture to the prepared loaf pan. If you are using a baking dish, form the chicken mixture into a loaf shape and carefully transfer it to the prepared baking dish. Cover the meatloaf with aluminum foil, then bake it for 30 minutes.

While the meatloaf is baking, combine the tomato sauce, brown sugar, Worcestershire sauce, onion powder, ground mustard, remaining 1 teaspoon of black pepper and remaining ½ teaspoon of Himalayan pink salt in a small saucepan over medium heat. Stir the ingredients together. Cook the barbecue glaze for 5 minutes, stirring it occasionally, until the ingredients are well combined and the sauce is smooth. Remove the saucepan from the heat.

Cover the chicken meatloaf evenly with the barbecue glaze and bake the meatloaf, uncovered, for 15 minutes, until the meatloaf's internal temperature reaches 165°F (74°C) and the glaze is slightly caramelized. Remove the meatloaf from the oven and allow it to cool for 10 minutes before serving it.

MOMMA PEARL'S POT ROAST

3 lb (1.4 kg) grass-fed beef chuck roast

2 tsp (4 g) dried oregano

2 tsp (6 g) garlic powder, divided

2 tsp (4 g) black pepper, divided

3 tsp (6 g) Himalayan pink salt, divided

3 tbsp (45 ml) olive oil

1 cup (160 g) coarsely chopped white onion

¼ cup (36 g) minced garlic

2 tbsp (16 g) arrowroot flour

1 cup (70 g) thickly sliced white button mushrooms

1 lb (454 g) red potatoes, cut in half

2 tsp (4 g) smoked paprika

1 tsp ground allspice

⅓ cup (80 ml) red wine

1 tbsp (15 ml) Worcestershire sauce

3½ cups (840 ml) low-sodium beef stock

1 dried bay leaf

When it comes to Sunday supper, nothing beats a classic pot roast! When I was growing up, my family came to know it as a lazy Sunday meal. It was an approachable meal for my family that didn't require an expensive cut of meat. As a matter of fact, it's made with the opposite. Pot roast made with chuck roast is the definition of turning something good into something extraordinary. With this recipe, you have a complete meal since the veggies are cooked right along with your meat. How simple is that? If you want to serve it with sides, though, try serving it with Creamy Mashed Potatoes (page 125) or Southern Green Beans and Potatoes (page 126).

Once you sear the meat and place all of the ingredients into your Dutch oven, it will slowly cook for several hours. As the roast settles, the vegetables will appear after being freed from the weight of the hearty roast. The rich gravy is present in every bite, and the tender, firm red potatoes and carrots are just as tasty as the succulent meat.

To make this recipe healthier, I use grass-fed and low-sodium beef stock. And let's not forget about the red wine, which is rich in antioxidants, regulates cholesterol levels and keeps the heart healthy. This savory roast is easy to make and a perfect way to feed the entire family. Plus, you'll have plenty of leftovers for a few more meals!

Preheat the oven to 300°F (149°C).

Season the beef chuck roast evenly with the oregano, 1 teaspoon of the garlic powder, 1 teaspoon of the black pepper and 1 teaspoon of the Himalayan pink salt. Set the roast aside.

Heat a 7½-quart (7.2-L) Dutch oven over high heat, and then add the olive oil. Sear the beef chuck roast for 2 minutes on each side, then remove the roast from the Dutch oven. Reduce the heat to medium, then add the onion and minced garlic to the Dutch oven. Cook the onion and garlic for 5 minutes. Add the arrowroot flour and cook the mixture, stirring it constantly, for 1 to 2 minutes, until it begins to thicken. Add the mushrooms and cook the mixture for 2 to 3 minutes.

(continued)

MOMMA PEARL'S POT ROAST (CONT.)

Add the red potatoes, smoked paprika, allspice, remaining 1 teaspoon of garlic powder, remaining 1 teaspoon of black pepper and remaining 2 teaspoons (4 g) of Himalayan pink salt. Stir the ingredients to combine them. Pour the red wine, Worcestershire sauce and beef stock into the Dutch oven and bring the mixture to a gentle boil.

Return the roast to the Dutch oven and top the roast with the bay leaf. Cover the Dutch oven, place it in the oven and bake the roast for 3 hours and 30 minutes, until the meat is tender and easily falls apart. Remove the Dutch oven from the oven and allow the pot roast to cool, covered, for 30 minutes before serving it.

LOW-FAT OLD-FASHIONED CHICKEN AND DUMPLINGS

1 cup (125 g) all-purpose flour, plus more as needed

1 tsp Himalayan pink salt, divided

¼ tsp baking powder

¼ cup (57 g) cold unsalted butter, diced

6 tbsp (75 ml) 2% milk

1 tsp fresh lemon juice

4½ cups (1.1 L) low-sodium chicken broth

1 lb (454 g) boneless, skinless chicken breasts

½ tsp celery salt

½ tsp ground cumin

2 tbsp (30 ml) olive oil

1 cup (160 g) coarsely chopped white onion

¼ cup (25 g) coarsely chopped celery

1 tbsp plus 2 tsp (15 g) minced garlic

1 cup (145 g) frozen peas

¼ cup (15 g) coarsely chopped fresh parsley

1 tsp black pepper

1 tsp ground thyme

1 tsp rubbed sage

1 tsp Creole seasoning

½ tsp pure ground gumbo filé

½ tsp garlic powder

¼ tsp cayenne pepper

1 cup (240 ml) canned light coconut milk

Chicken and dumplings is a classic southern comfort food that has been around for ages. A thick stew loaded with simple veggies, tender shredded chicken and flat, pillowy southern-style dumplings that soak up the richness of the stew—it's completely satisfying and downright comforting.

With a few simple tweaks, you can easily transform this usually heavy dish into something better for you. It all starts with making your dumplings from scratch with healthier ingredients, which is an immediate win—plus, it results in softer, chewier dumplings. Next, you can reduce the sodium by using a low-sodium broth, and you can control the amount of fat by subbing coconut milk for heavy cream or evaporated milk. Finally, this healthier take on the classic uses a simple kitchen hack to create a buttermilk substitute with two very common ingredients: milk and lemon.

Chicken and dumplings has a history. This dish has brought many people through some of the roughest times in their lives. Enjoy it with family and friends and see how it warms the soul.

To make the dumplings, put the flour, ½ teaspoon of the Himalayan pink salt and baking powder in a medium bowl. Stir the ingredients with a fork until they are combined. Add the butter to the bowl and use a pastry cutter to combine it with the flour until small crumbs appear in the mixture. Set the flour mixture aside.

In a small bowl, combine the milk and lemon juice to make "buttermilk." Add the buttermilk to the flour mixture. Using your hands, gently mix the dough until it binds together.

Dust a work surface with flour, then transfer the dough to the prepared work surface and knead the dough 5 or 6 times. Dust the work surface with additional flour as needed. Using a floured rolling pin, roll out the dough until it's about ¼ inch (6 mm) thick. Use a pizza cutter to cut the dough into strips that are 1½ inches (4 cm) wide and 6 inches (15 cm) long. Allow the dumplings to rest on the counter for 30 minutes.

(continued)

LOW-FAT OLD-FASHIONED CHICKEN AND DUMPLINGS (CONT.)

In an 8-quart (7.7-L) saucepan over high heat, bring the chicken broth to a boil. Add the chicken breasts to the saucepan and boil them for 10 minutes. Remove the chicken from the broth, transfer it to a cutting board and shred it with a fork. Note that the chicken may still be pink after boiling; however, the chicken will cook completely in a later step.

Transfer the shredded chicken to a clean medium bowl, and then season it with the celery salt and cumin. Set the shredded chicken aside. Pour the broth from the saucepan into a large bowl to use in the next step.

Reduce the heat to medium and return the saucepan to the heat. Add the olive oil, onion, celery and minced garlic to the saucepan. Cook the vegetables for 5 minutes. Add the peas, parsley, black pepper, thyme, sage, Creole seasoning, gumbo filé, garlic powder, cayenne pepper, remaining ½ teaspoon of Himalayan pink salt, coconut milk and chicken broth to the vegetables. Bring the mixture to a gentle boil.

Gently add the dumplings, one at a time, to the stew. Reduce the heat to medium-low, cover the saucepan and cook the stew and dumplings for 8 minutes. Gently fold in the shredded chicken. Reduce the heat to low, cover the saucepan and cook the chicken and dumplings for 10 minutes, until the dumplings are tender and the chicken is completely opaque all the way through.

LOW-FAT CREOLE FISH ÉTOUFFÉE

2 lb (908 g) fresh skinless cod loin fillets

1 tsp smoked paprika

1 tsp dried basil

1 tsp black pepper, divided

¼ cup (57 g) unsalted butter

¼ cup (60 ml) olive oil

½ cup (80 g) coarsely chopped white onion

½ cup (51 g) coarsely chopped celery

½ cup (75 g) coarsely chopped green bell pepper

½ cup (25 g) coarsely chopped green onion, divided

¼ cup (36 g) minced garlic

¼ cup (31 g) all-purpose flour

¾ cup (198 g) tomato paste

2 cups (360 g) diced tomatoes, drained

1 tbsp (5 g) Creole seasoning

¼ tsp cayenne pepper

½ tsp Himalayan pink salt

2 cups (480 ml) low-sodium chicken broth

This dish combines the creamy consistency of an étouffée with the vibrant flavors of a tomato-based Creole stew. I take Cajun étouffée, with its nutty roux, a step further by incorporating tomatoes, resulting in a creamy tomato-based stew—and that's where the Creole aspect comes into play. Creole cuisine uses tomatoes as a primary ingredient, while Cajun cuisine traditionally does not. A rich, tomato-based stew is more characteristic of Creole food. This dish is one of my favorite ways to combine flavors from both cultures.

Many times, you find recipes like this use crawfish or shrimp. However, if you are allergic to shellfish or choose not to eat shellfish for dietary restrictions, this recipe is right up your alley. You still get to enjoy all the flavors you are looking for with a slight adjustment. Flaky chunks of cod and layers of fresh ingredients—including the holy trinity of onions, celery and bell peppers—intertwine in a rich, buttery and spicy sauce with few calories and little fat but all the flavors. Serve it over rice for an authentic Cajun meal!

Cut the cod fillets into large chunks, then season the chunks with the smoked paprika, basil and ½ teaspoon of the black pepper.

Heat a 4-quart (3.8-L) sauté pan over medium heat, then add the butter and olive oil. Add the white onion, celery, bell pepper, ⅜ cup (19 g) green onion and garlic to the sauté pan. Cook the vegetables for 2 minutes, then add the flour and cook the mixture, stirring it constantly for 2 to 3 minutes.

Add the tomato paste, diced tomatoes, Creole seasoning, cayenne pepper, Himalayan pink salt and remaining ½ teaspoon of black pepper. Stir the ingredients together, then add the chicken broth. Bring the mixture to a gentle boil, add the cod and reduce the heat to medium-low. Cook the stew, covered, for 10 to 12 minutes, until the stew is bubbling and the cod is opaque all the way through. Add the remaining ⅛ cup (6 g) of green onion on top of the stew before serving.

CHICKEN AND CHICKEN SAUSAGE JAMBALAYA

1 cup (200 g) long-grain brown rice

1 lb (454 g) boneless, skinless chicken breasts

1 tsp paprika

½ tsp ground thyme

13 oz (364 g) chicken sausage with beef casing, thinly sliced

2 tbsp (30 ml) olive oil

1 tbsp (9 g) minced garlic

1 cup (160 g) coarsely chopped red onion

½ cup (51 g) coarsely chopped celery

1 cup (149 g) coarsely chopped green bell pepper

2 cups (360 g) fire-roasted diced tomatoes, drained

2 tbsp (10 g) Creole seasoning

1 tsp black pepper

1 tsp dried basil

1 tsp garlic powder

1 tsp dried oregano

½ tsp white pepper

¼ tsp cayenne pepper

This jambalaya is a one-pot meal made with ingredients you likely already have. Swapping out the protein and replacing the usual white rice with brown rice means this meal is quick, easy and better for you.

Made with a hearty portion of tender chicken breast and juicy chicken sausage, this dish is filled with Creole flavors and even packs a little heat. Grab a few simple ingredients and the holy trinity—a simple blend of onions, bell peppers and celery—and you are good to go. Don't worry, you won't need any sides—this dish is the perfect solo artist.

In a 2-quart (1.9-L) saucepan, cook the brown rice according to the package's instructions. Set the cooked rice aside.

While the rice is cooking, cut the chicken breasts into medium cubes. Season them with the paprika and thyme. Heat a 5-quart (4.8-L) sauté pan over medium heat. Add the chicken and sauté it for 3 minutes, or until it is completely opaque all the way through. Remove the chicken from the heat and set it aside.

Set the sauté pan over medium-high heat. Add the chicken sausage and cook it for 5 minutes, or until it is browned. Remove the sausage from the pan and set it aside.

Reduce the heat to medium and set the sauté pan over the heat. Add the olive oil, minced garlic, onion, celery and bell pepper. Cook the vegetables for 5 minutes, stirring them occasionally, until all the vegetables are soft and the onion is translucent.

Add the diced tomatoes, chicken breast, chicken sausage and brown rice to the vegetable mixture. Stir the ingredients to combine them well. Fold in the Creole seasoning, black pepper, basil, garlic powder, oregano, white pepper and cayenne pepper. Reduce the heat to low, cover the sauté pan and cook the jambalaya for 10 minutes, until it is warmed through.

YIELD: 4 SERVINGS

1 lb (454 g) beef sausage with beef casing, thickly sliced

1 tbsp (15 ml) olive oil

1 cup (172 g) canned baby lima beans

½ tsp Himalayan pink salt

1 lb (454 g) fresh or frozen whole okra

1 cup (136 g) frozen corn kernels

2 cups (360 g) fire-roasted crushed tomatoes, drained

2 tbsp (18 g) minced garlic

½ cup (120 ml) low-sodium chicken stock

2 tsp (4 g) Creole seasoning

1 tsp paprika

1 tsp ground thyme

1 tsp black pepper

½ tsp garlic powder

¼ tsp cayenne pepper

CREOLE OKRA AND TOMATOES WITH BEEF SAUSAGE

This recipe takes me to those special moments I spent with my grandmother, whom we called Grams. She would always make this dish on Sundays after church. I'm still amazed at how much I enjoyed it, because I was not too fond of vegetables as a kid. Recipes like this changed my mind.

To put my spin on my grandmother's recipe, I combined two classics—succotash and stewed okra and tomatoes. Succotash uses sliced okra, sweet corn, lima beans and tomatoes, and stewed okra and tomatoes is a vibrant yet straightforward pairing of whole okra and tomatoes in a tangy tomato sauce.

My healthier twist swaps pork sausage for juicy beef sausage, which adds depth and dimension to this dish. Plus, I include twice the amount of veggies compared to the traditional preparation. This recipe is so good, it can make anyone forget how light it is.

In a 10-inch (25-cm) cast-iron skillet over high heat, cook the beef sausage for 5 minutes, until it is browned. Remove the beef sausage from the skillet and set the sausage aside.

In the same skillet, combine the olive oil, lima beans and Himalayan salt. Reduce the heat to medium and cook the mixture, covered, for 5 minutes. Add the okra, corn, crushed tomatoes, minced garlic, beef sausage, chicken stock, Creole seasoning, paprika, thyme, black pepper, garlic powder and cayenne pepper. Stir the ingredients to combine them well. Cover the skillet and cook the mixture for 15 minutes, until the vegetables are tender.

LOW-SODIUM NEW ORLEANS–STYLE BLACKENED SALMON

BLACKENED SALMON

3 lb (1.4 kg) fresh skin-on salmon fillets

1 tbsp (6 g) paprika

1 tbsp (6 g) chili powder

1 tsp garlic powder

½ tsp black pepper

½ tsp dried thyme

½ tsp dried oregano

½ tsp cayenne pepper

1 tsp Creole seasoning

½ tsp onion powder

1 tsp dried basil

½ tsp Himalayan pink salt

1 tsp olive oil

LEMON-PARMESAN SAUCE

1 tbsp (14 g) unsalted butter

1 cup (240 ml) canned light coconut milk

1 cup (100 g) grated Parmesan cheese

1 tsp lemon-pepper seasoning

1 tsp dried basil

¼ tsp Himalayan pink salt

1 tbsp (9 g) minced garlic

I wouldn't be surprised if this recipe became your favorite way to enjoy salmon. It's easy to make, perfectly seasoned and drizzled with a lemon-Parmesan sauce, because that's probably the only thing that could make this blackened salmon any better. The popular technique of blackening seafood has deep Cajun roots, and as with everything I prepare, it's all about the herbs and seasonings.

At the core of this blackened salmon recipe, you'll find thyme, oregano and other pantry staples like garlic powder, paprika and even cayenne pepper, which brings the heat. After the salmon is rubbed generously with seasonings, it spends some time in a hot cast-iron skillet until the fish is blackened, resulting in intensely flavored fish with a slightly charred exterior.

The key to making this meal healthier is choosing a protein high in nutrients, swapping high-calorie ingredients for those with fewer calories and skipping the store-bought seasonings. For this recipe, I use salmon, which is high in omega-3 fatty acids. I also swap heavy cream for coconut milk to reduce the fat and make the blackened seasoning at home to control the amount of sodium.

To make the blackened salmon, preheat the oven to 400°F (204°C). Lightly grease a large cast-iron skillet.

Cut the salmon fillets into four 3-inch (7.5-cm)-thick portions. Season the salmon evenly with the paprika, chili powder, garlic powder, black pepper, thyme, oregano, cayenne pepper, Creole seasoning, onion powder, basil and Himalayan pink salt. Lightly coat each piece of salmon with the olive oil. Place the salmon on the prepared skillet and bake it for 8 minutes. For medium-rare to medium salmon, the internal temperature should range between 125 and 135°F (52 and 57°C). Remove the salmon from the oven and set it aside.

To make the lemon-Parmesan sauce, heat a small saucepan over medium heat. Add the butter and allow it to melt. Add the coconut milk, Parmesan cheese, lemon-pepper seasoning, basil, Himalayan pink salt and minced garlic, and then stir to combine the ingredients. Reduce the heat to low and cook the sauce for 5 minutes, stirring it occasionally.

Top the blackened salmon with the lemon-Parmesan sauce and serve it.

BOURBON-BRAISED SHORT RIBS

If you have yet to enjoy bone-in braised short ribs, you are missing out! This recipe makes it easy to reduce the carbs and up the protein in your diet—well, that's if you are counting.

These short ribs are slow-cooked until they are fork-tender, and they are braised in an aromatic blend of bourbon (which adds a rich, robust flavor and tenderizes the meat), low-sodium beef stock and just enough light brown sugar to create a not-too-sweet glaze.

A single short rib is plenty for an individual portion. Serve each rib on top of my Creamy Mashed Potatoes (page 125), with the very sauce the short ribs were braised in—oh me, oh my! These ribs are fall-off-the-bone good.

2–3 lb (908 g–1.4 kg) short ribs

3 tsp (6 g) Himalayan pink salt, divided

3 tsp (6 g) black pepper, divided

2 tsp (6 g) garlic powder, divided

1 tsp dried oregano

2 tbsp (16 g) all-purpose flour

⅓ cup (80 ml) olive oil

1 cup (160 g) coarsely chopped white onion

3 tbsp (27 g) minced garlic

2 tbsp (32 g) tomato paste

⅓ cup (73 g) light brown sugar

2 tsp (2 g) rubbed sage

1 tsp ground thyme

½ tsp dried marjoram

½ tsp onion powder

1 cup (240 ml) bourbon

3 cups (720 ml) low-sodium beef broth

3 sprigs fresh rosemary

Preheat the oven to 300°F (149°C).

Season the short ribs evenly with 2 teaspoons (4 g) of the Himalayan pink salt, 2 teaspoons (4 g) of the black pepper, 1 teaspoon of the garlic powder and oregano. Lightly coat the short ribs with the flour.

Heat a 7½-quart (7.2-L) Dutch oven over high heat. Add the olive oil, and then add the short ribs and sear them for 2 minutes on each side. Remove the short ribs from the Dutch oven. Reduce the heat to medium and add the onion and minced garlic. Cook the mixture for 5 minutes, stirring it occasionally.

Add the tomato paste, brown sugar, sage, thyme, marjoram, onion powder, remaining 1 teaspoon of Himalayan pink salt, remaining 1 teaspoon of black pepper and remaining 1 teaspoon of garlic powder. Stir to combine the ingredients. Pour in the bourbon and beef broth. Bring the broth to a gentle boil, then add short ribs. Add the rosemary sprigs and cover the Dutch oven.

Bake the short ribs for 1 hour. Reduce the heat to 275°F (135°C) and cook the short ribs for an additional 2 hours. Allow the short ribs to cool, covered, for 30 minutes before serving them.

BAKED BARBECUE CHICKEN THIGHS

2–3 lb (908 g –1.4 kg) bone-in, skin-on chicken thighs

2 tsp (4 g) paprika

2 tsp (4 g) black pepper, divided

1½ tsp (3 g) Himalayan pink salt, divided

1 tsp garlic powder, divided

2 cups (480 ml) tomato puree

½ cup (110 g) brown sugar

2 tbsp (30 ml) Worcestershire sauce

2 tbsp (30 ml) apple cider vinegar

1 tbsp (9 g) minced garlic

1 tbsp (6 g) chili powder

½ tsp onion powder

You get a pass for licking your fingers after you sink your teeth into these slightly sweet and sticky glazed barbecue chicken thighs! You get all that goodness without having to go near a grill—and that's not always a bad thing. It makes this recipe perfect for whenever you want tender, juicy chicken—no matter the season.

Even though these bone-in chicken thighs are oven-baked, they don't dry out. They turn out juicy every single time. But the simple and quick sauce is the secret to this barbecue chicken recipe. The sauce creates a thick, sticky, sweet and smoky layer of perfection. The best barbecue sauce is the one you make yourself—and when you make your sauce at home, you can keep those calories and refined sugars in check.

Preheat the oven to 400°F (204°C). Lightly grease a large nonstick baking sheet.

Season the chicken thighs evenly with the paprika, 1 teaspoon of the black pepper, 1 teaspoon of the Himalayan pink salt and ½ teaspoon of the garlic powder. Place the chicken thighs, skin side down, on the prepared baking sheet. Cover the baking sheet with aluminum foil and bake the chicken thighs for 25 minutes.

While the chicken thighs are baking, combine the tomato puree, brown sugar, Worcestershire sauce, apple cider vinegar, minced garlic, chili powder, onion powder, remaining 1 teaspoon of black pepper, remaining ½ teaspoon of Himalayan pink salt and remaining ½ teaspoon of garlic powder in a 2-quart (1.9-L) saucepan. Stir the ingredients together well, then bring the sauce to a gentle boil over medium heat. Reduce the heat to low, cover the saucepan and cook the sauce for 5 minutes. Remove the saucepan from the heat.

Uncover the baking sheet and flip the chicken thighs over so that the skin is facing up. Cover the chicken thighs with barbecue sauce. Bake the chicken, uncovered, for 25 minutes, then remove the baking sheet from the oven. Set the oven to broil, then return the baking sheet to the oven and broil the chicken for 1 to 2 minutes, until the thighs are slightly charred and the sauce creates a thick glaze. Remove the chicken from the oven. Let the chicken cool for 5 to 10 minutes before serving it.

LOWER-CALORIE SMOTHERED CHICKEN WITH BROWN GRAVY

2–3 lb (908 g–1.4 kg) chicken drumsticks and wings

1½ tsp (3 g) Himalayan pink salt, divided

1½ tsp (5 g) garlic powder, divided

1 tsp dried oregano

1½ tsp (3 g) black pepper, divided

½ tsp onion powder

½ cup plus 3 tbsp (87 g) all-purpose flour, divided

⅓ cup (80 ml) olive oil

1 cup (130 g) thinly sliced white onion

3 tbsp (27 g) minced garlic

1 tsp smoked paprika

½ tsp ground thyme

3 cups (720 ml) low-sodium chicken stock

Chicken simmering in its own juices, smothered in brown gravy and surrounded by sliced white onions—it's the one-pot meal that deserves a place on your table.

The tender meat falls right off the bone, and the velvety onion-laced gravy (prepared like a light roux using low-sodium chicken stock) is perfectly at home when placed on a bed of rice. You can also serve it with your favorite vegetables. And while this recipe is a little different than the smothered fried chicken I looked forward to as a child, I've made it even healthier by using olive oil and less flour to minimize the carbs.

Preheat the oven to 400°F (204°C).

Season the chicken legs and wings evenly with 1 teaspoon of the Himalayan pink salt, 1 teaspoon of the garlic powder, oregano, ½ teaspoon of the black pepper and onion powder. Place ½ cup (63 g) of the flour in a large ziplock bag, then add the chicken and toss to coat it with the flour.

Heat an 8-quart (7.7-L) ovenproof sauté pan over high heat, then add the olive oil. Sear the chicken for 1 to 2 minutes per side, then remove the chicken from the sauté pan.

Reduce the heat to medium, and then add the onion and minced garlic. Cook the vegetables for 5 minutes, until the onion is translucent. Add the remaining 3 tablespoons (24 g) of flour to the sauté pan and stir it together with the onion and garlic, until it forms a thick paste. Add the smoked paprika, thyme, remaining ½ teaspoon of Himalayan pink salt, remaining ½ teaspoon of garlic powder and remaining 1 teaspoon of black pepper. Allow the mixture to cook for 3 minutes, stirring it constantly, or until it has thickened slightly.

Pour the chicken stock into the sauté pan and bring the mixture to a gentle boil, then add the chicken back to the sauté pan and cover the pan.

Bake the chicken and gravy for 25 minutes, or until the chicken's internal temperature reaches 165°F (74°C) and its juices run clear when the meat is cut. Remove the sauté pan from the oven and allow the chicken and gravy to cool slightly before serving.

LOW-SODIUM VEGETARIAN CREOLE RISOTTO

2 tbsp (28 g) unsalted butter

1 cup (160 g) coarsely chopped white onion

½ cup (75 g) coarsely chopped green bell pepper

½ cup (51 g) coarsely chopped celery

3 tbsp (27 g) minced garlic

2½ cups (175 g) coarsely chopped cremini mushrooms

½ cup (30 g) finely chopped fresh parsley

1¼ cups (250 g) Arborio rice

2 tsp (4 g) Creole seasoning

1 tsp dried basil

1 tsp ground thyme

1 tsp black pepper

½ tsp ground allspice

½ tsp Himalayan pink salt

2 cups (360 g) fire-roasted diced tomatoes, drained

¼ cup (60 ml) white wine

3 cups (720 ml) canned light coconut milk, divided

2 cups (480 ml) low-sodium vegetable stock

1 cup (100 g) grated Parmesan cheese

1 tbsp (15 ml) hot sauce

Just when you thought risotto couldn't get any better, I combined it with Creole flavors, roasted tomatoes, mushrooms and the holy trinity—a flavorful combination of onion, celery and green bell pepper—to share a creamy vegetable version perfect for Meatless Monday.

While risotto can be a labor of love and is typically simmered on the stove to create the fluffy and silky texture we thoroughly enjoy, I have a perfect method for those of you who want the same results in less time. Twenty minutes in the oven and the Arborio rice is soft and creamy, and it makes for a complete meal in a bowl. This risotto is comforting, cozy, rich and indulgent in the best way possible. It delivers all the comfort-food vibes while ingredients like low-sodium vegetable stock, coconut milk and fresh vegetables keep things light. This recipe will be your new way to risotto.

Preheat the oven to 400°F (204°C).

Heat a 5-quart (4.8-L) ovenproof sauté pan over medium heat. Add the butter, onion, bell pepper, celery and garlic. Cook the vegetables for 5 minutes. Add the mushrooms and parsley and cook the mixture for 2 minutes.

Move half the mixture to one side of the pan and the other half of the mixture to the other side, then add the Arborio rice, Creole seasoning, basil, thyme, black pepper, allspice and Himalayan pink salt. Cook the mixture for 1 minute, stirring it occasionally. Add the diced tomatoes and white wine. Stir the ingredients together, then add 2 cups (480 ml) of the coconut milk and the vegetable stock. Bring the rice to a boil.

Cover the sauté pan and bake the rice for 20 minutes. Remove the sauté pan from the oven, and then fold the remaining 1 cup (240 ml) of coconut milk, Parmesan cheese and hot sauce into the baked Arborio rice. Serve the risotto immediately.

SEARED HALIBUT WITH SUCCOTASH

HALIBUT

1½–2 lb (681–908 g) fresh skin-on halibut fillets

1 tsp Creole seasoning

½ tsp black pepper

1 tsp dried parsley

½ tsp Himalayan pink salt

3 tbsp (45 ml) olive oil, divided

SUCCOTASH

2 tbsp (30 ml) olive oil

3 tbsp (27 g) minced garlic

1 lb (454 g) frozen cut okra

2 cups (272 g) frozen corn kernels

1 cup (172 g) frozen lima beans

2 cups (360 g) fire-roasted diced tomatoes, drained

2 tsp (4 g) ground thyme

1 tsp Creole seasoning

1 tsp garlic powder

1 tsp black pepper

½ tsp Himalayan pink salt

¼ tsp cayenne pepper

I didn't get to enjoy a lot of halibut growing up. It was one fish my family reserved for special occasions, and if I was lucky, I would get my fill during family celebrations when we had the chance to eat out. What was an infrequent encounter back then, I can make up for now—and boy, do I.

My simply seasoned, flaky fish joins succotash—a vibrant blend of corn, okra, lima beans and diced tomatoes. This light, flavorful and perfectly paired duo will leave you satisfied without the guilt!

To make the halibut, season the fillets evenly with the Creole seasoning, black pepper, parsley and Himalayan pink salt. Coat the fillets with 1 tablespoon (15 ml) of the olive oil, then press the herbs and seasonings into the fish.

Heat the remaining 2 tablespoons (30 ml) of olive oil in a 12-inch (30-cm) skillet over medium heat. Add the halibut and cook it for 4 minutes on each side, until it flakes easily, is opaque and reaches an internal temperature of 145°F (63°C).

To make the succotash, heat a 5-quart (4.8-L) sauté pan over medium heat, then add the olive oil and minced garlic. Cook the garlic for 1 to 2 minutes. Add the okra, corn, lima beans, diced tomatoes, thyme, Creole seasoning, garlic powder, black pepper, Himalayan pink salt and cayenne pepper. Stir to combine the ingredients well, then cook the succotash for 20 minutes, until the beans have softened.

To serve, transfer the succotash to a serving dish and top it with the halibut fillets.

LOW-SODIUM CHICKEN-FRIED CHICKEN WITH COUNTRY GRAVY

1 lb (454 g) boneless, skinless chicken breasts

2 tsp (4 g) smoked paprika

3 tsp (6 g) black pepper, divided

1½ tsp (5 g) garlic powder, divided

1 tsp chili powder

2 tsp (4 g) Himalayan pink salt, divided

½ tsp ground thyme

¼ tsp cayenne pepper

2 large eggs

½ cup (120 ml) canned light coconut milk

1 tbsp (15 ml) Sriracha sauce

2¼ cups (281 g) all-purpose flour, divided

2 tbsp (16 g) cornstarch

1 tsp baking powder

2 cups plus 2 tbsp (510 ml) sunflower oil

2 tbsp (28 g) unsalted butter

1 tbsp (9 g) minced garlic

2 cups (480 ml) 2% milk

1 tbsp (6 g) grated Parmesan cheese

1 tsp dried oregano

½ tsp onion powder

"No, not chicken-fried steak. Chicken-fried chicken." I can't tell you how many times I've had to repeat this, as if others are in denial that chicken-fried chicken is a thing. Well, in the South, it is a huge thing. While this recipe is a variation of the traditional chicken-fried steak, I may be a little biased and will admittedly call this my favorite of the two. On top of the fact that it tastes great, this easy protein swap is healthier.

Crispy and juicy butterflied chicken breasts are battered using light coconut milk instead of buttermilk then pan-fried in just enough sunflower oil to ensure the chicken is perfectly golden. The gravy is thick and can hold its own, yet made with lighter ingredients, so it doesn't weigh you down. And then the two come together; it is southern cooking at its finest. Serve with a side of my Creamy Mashed Potatoes (page 125) or Southern Green Beans and Potatoes (page 126) for a complete meal. Dinner never tasted so good!

Cut each of the chicken breasts in half. Cover the chicken with plastic wrap, and lightly pound it with a meat tenderizer until it is ½ inch (1.3 cm) thick. Season the chicken evenly with the smoked paprika, 2 teaspoons (4 g) of the black pepper, 1 teaspoon of the garlic powder, chili powder, 1 teaspoon of the Himalayan pink salt, thyme and cayenne pepper.

In a large bowl, mix together the eggs, coconut milk and Sriracha sauce. Submerge the chicken into the egg mixture. Allow the chicken to marinate for 15 minutes in the refrigerator.

In a large ziplock bag, combine 2 cups (250 g) of the flour, ½ teaspoon of the Himalayan pink salt, cornstarch and baking powder. Place the marinated chicken breasts in the flour mixture. Close the bag, shake it well to coat the chicken and then place it in the refrigerator for 15 minutes.

Heat 2 cups (480 ml) of the sunflower oil in a deep 12-inch (30-cm) skillet over medium-high heat. Preheat the oven to 175°F (79°C).

(continued)

Add the chicken to the skillet and pan-fry it for 4 minutes on each side, until it is golden brown and crispy and its internal temperature reaches 165°F (74°C). Transfer the fried chicken to a large nonstick baking sheet, then place the baking sheet in the oven to keep the chicken warm while you make the gravy.

Next, heat a 2-quart (1.9-L) saucepan over medium heat. Add the remaining 2 tablespoons (30 ml) of sunflower oil and the butter. Once the butter has melted, add the minced garlic and cook it for 1 minute. Stir in the remaining ¼ cup (31 g) flour to form a thick paste, then add the milk. Stirring the mixture constantly, add the Parmesan cheese, oregano, onion powder, remaining 1 teaspoon of black pepper, remaining ½ teaspoon garlic powder and remaining ½ teaspoon of Himalayan pink salt. Reduce the temperature to low and cook the gravy for 8 to 10 minutes, until it is thick and silky.

To serve, pour the gravy over the chicken or serve the chicken with the gravy on the side.

LOW-SODIUM HEALTHIER SALISBURY STEAK

8 oz (224 g) lean ground beef

8 oz (224 g) lean ground turkey

3 cups (210 g) thickly sliced cremini mushrooms, divided

1 cup (160 g) coarsely chopped white onion, divided

½ cup (50 g) grated Parmesan cheese

¼ cup (14 g) panko breadcrumbs

1 large egg

2 tbsp (30 ml) tomato puree, divided

3 tbsp (27 g) minced garlic, divided

1 tbsp plus 1 tsp (20 ml) Worcestershire sauce, divided

3 tsp (15 ml) Dijon mustard, divided

1½ tsp (3 g) dried oregano, divided

1 tsp dried basil

1 tsp rubbed sage

2 tsp (4 g) black pepper, divided

2 tsp (4 g) Himalayan pink salt, divided

1 tsp paprika, divided

½ tsp garlic powder

¾ tsp ground thyme, divided

3 tbsp (45 ml) olive oil, divided

2 tbsp (16 g) all-purpose flour

½ tsp onion powder

⅛ tsp ground mustard

¼ cup (15 g) coarsely chopped fresh parsley

2 cups (480 ml) low-sodium beef broth

⅓ cup (80 ml) light sour cream

Salisbury steak gets a healthy upgrade when lean ground beef and turkey intertwine to lighten up this classic. My easy recipe is so rich and savory, you'd never guess that it's better for you.

My juicy Salisbury steak is smothered in a rich mushroom and onion gravy made with a low-sodium beef broth, Worcestershire sauce and light sour cream. Less fat and fewer calories than the beef-only version—but just as tasty—this version gives you more of what you need and less of what you don't. Serve this recipe with my Creamy Mashed Potatoes (page 125), or pair it with my Southern Green Beans and Potatoes (page 126).

In a large bowl, combine the ground beef and ground turkey.

Place ½ cup (35 g) of the chopped mushrooms and ½ cup (80 g) of the chopped onion in a food processor and pulse until they are minced. Add the mushroom-onion mixture to the beef and turkey. Add the Parmesan cheese, panko breadcrumbs, egg, 1 tablespoon (15 ml) of the tomato puree, 1 tablespoon (9 g) of the minced garlic, 1 teaspoon of the Worcestershire sauce, 2 teaspoons (10 ml) of the Dijon mustard, 1 teaspoon of the oregano, basil, sage, 1 teaspoon of the black pepper, 1 teaspoon of the Himalayan pink salt, ½ teaspoon of the paprika, garlic powder and ¼ teaspoon of the thyme. Mix until the ingredients are well combined. Form the meat mixture into 4-ounce (112-g) patties, then set the patties aside.

Heat a 12-inch (30-cm) sauté pan over high heat. Sear each patty for 1 minute on each side, and then remove the patty from the heat. Reduce the heat to medium, then add 1 tablespoon (15 ml) of olive oil and the remaining ½ cup (80 g) of chopped onion to the sauté pan. Cook the onion for 5 minutes, then add the remaining 2 tablespoons (30 ml) of olive oil and the flour, stirring the mixture constantly until a thick paste forms.

(continued)

LOW-SODIUM HEALTHIER SALISBURY STEAK (CONT.)

Add the remaining 2½ cups (175 g) of chopped mushrooms and cook the mixture for 2 to 3 minutes. Add the remaining 2 tablespoons (18 g) of minced garlic, remaining 1 tablespoon (15 ml) of tomato puree, remaining 1 tablespoon (15 ml) of Worcestershire sauce, remaining 1 teaspoon of Dijon mustard, remaining ½ teaspoon of oregano, remaining 1 teaspoon of black pepper, remaining 1 teaspoon of Himalayan pink salt, ½ teaspoon of paprika, ½ teaspoon of thyme, onion powder and ground mustard. Stir the ingredients together, then add the parsley and beef broth.

Bring the sauce to a gentle boil, then place the cooked patties in the sauce. Cover the patties with the sauce, reduce the heat to medium, cover the sauté pan and cook the patties for 8 to 10 minutes, until their internal temperature reaches 160°F (71°C).

Remove the sauté pan from the heat and add the sour cream to the sauce, folding it into the sauce carefully. Serve the Salisbury steak and sauce immediately.

RED SNAPPER AND CHEESE POLENTA WITH CREOLE TOMATOES

POLENTA

2 cups (480 ml) low-sodium chicken stock

2 cups (480 ml) evaporated milk

1 tsp Himalayan pink salt

1 cup (156 g) yellow cornmeal polenta

1 tbsp (14 g) unsalted butter

¼ cup (25 g) grated Parmesan cheese

1 cup (113 g) shredded sharp white Cheddar cheese

CREOLE TOMATOES

¼ cup (60 ml) olive oil

2 tbsp (28 g) unsalted butter

⅓ cup (12 g) coarsely chopped fresh basil

3 tbsp (27 g) minced garlic

2 cups (360 g) fire-roasted diced tomatoes, drained

¼ tsp red pepper flakes

½ tsp garlic powder

¼ tsp Himalayan pink salt

⅛ tsp cayenne pepper

RED SNAPPER

2 lb (908 g) skin-on red snapper fillets

1 tsp Creole seasoning

½ tsp Himalayan pink salt

½ tsp black pepper

¼ tsp ground thyme

I don't know how I ever went through life without polenta! It's probably the coarse texture of the grain that I enjoy the most, but the fact that it's a good source of protein, fiber and complex carbohydrates is a bonus. This versatile side dish is even better when it's combined with other ingredients like low-sodium chicken stock, white Cheddar cheese and evaporated milk. Both the white Cheddar cheese and evaporated milk are great alternatives to the traditional yellow Cheddar cheese and heavy cream, respectively, as those items contain more fat overall. This cheesy polenta recipe is the only one you'll ever need.

I've paired cheesy polenta with a Creole-seasoned red snapper fillet to transform this fish into a meal that will knock your socks off. Both the snapper and polenta are topped with juicy fire-roasted tomatoes blended with fresh basil, garlic and red pepper flakes. The Creole tomatoes give the dish a new spin while balancing the savory polenta and adding a little kick to the mild red snapper. It tastes just as good as it looks.

To make the polenta, combine the chicken stock and evaporated milk in a 4-quart (3.8-L) saucepan. Bring the mixture to a boil over high heat. Add the Himalayan pink salt and polenta, stir the ingredients together and reduce the heat to low. Cover the saucepan and cook the polenta for 5 minutes, stirring it occasionally. Remove the saucepan from the heat, then add the butter, Parmesan cheese and Cheddar cheese. Stir the polenta until the cheeses have melted.

To make the Creole tomatoes, heat a 2-quart (1.9-L) saucepan over medium-low heat, then add the olive oil and butter. Once the butter has melted, add the basil, minced garlic, diced tomatoes, red pepper flakes, garlic powder, Himalayan pink salt and cayenne pepper. Cook the tomatoes for 5 minutes, stirring them occasionally, until they are warmed through.

To make the red snapper, season the fillets with the Creole seasoning, Himalayan pink salt, black pepper and thyme. Heat a 12-inch (30-cm) skillet over high heat. Add the red snapper fillets and cook them for 3 minutes on each side, until their internal temperature reaches 137°F (58°C) and they are opaque in color. Serve the fish over the polenta and topped with the Creole tomatoes.

SANDWICH SHOP

After learning how to form a patty and sear a juicy, well-seasoned burger on my own, my confidence in the kitchen grew, and it gave me a sense of independence at a young age. There was nothing like grilling a giant sandwich that resembled a Scooby Snack and challenging my cousins to an eating competition in the summertime. We would even pan-fry bologna until it bubbled into a mini dome, serve it between slices of white bread with mustard and then relish in the thought that we were chefs. My summers were the most memorable.

My cousins and I would ride our bikes everywhere, making frequent stops at the two local sandwich shops—one served up burgers while the other was the spot for po' boys. We were always able to gather enough money among the members of our group to order a double cheeseburger or seafood po' boy for everyone. In Louisiana, we learned quickly that one of the most essential parts of a sandwich is the bun. Having a soft, buttery bun on any sandwich would change a person's perspective on life.

Those experiences led me to be somewhat of a burger and sandwich connoisseur. Now that I'm not eating to gain weight for football, I try to make better decisions regarding the burgers and sandwiches I enjoy. (In high school, I once ate seven hamburgers on a bet, and those days are far behind me now. But I digress . . .)

The quality of the meat in my sandwiches has become more of a priority. Meats high in protein but low in fat are an important part of attaining a healthier lifestyle. And while cooking with leaner meats can be challenging due to their lower fat content, I've been able to find a good balance. When using ground meats, I incorporate other ingredients like eggs or Parmesan cheese. To keep my chicken breasts tender and juicy, I always tenderize my chicken during the preparation process. These minor tweaks are just a couple of examples of how you can prepare healthier burgers and sandwiches without losing a step in the taste department.

In this chapter, you will find a plethora of juicy, tender and flavorful burgers and sandwiches made with various proteins. For the seafood lovers, I created my Blackened BLT Fish Po' Boys (page 50), a spin on the traditional seafood po' boy—I converted it to a lightened-up fish sandwich in which flavorful blackened halibut is swapped for fried fish and topped off with crispy beef bacon. A few other must-haves are the lean yet juicy Bison Sliders with Caramelized Onions (page 67). The Veggie Muffuletta Sandwiches (page 55), with seared portobello mushrooms, melty provolone cheese and mind-blowing olive relish will satisfy even those who are skeptical about vegetables. And my Tender Pulled Short Rib Sandwiches (page 53), made with a homemade barbecue sauce, are a great option when you want healthier comfort food.

Welcome to my neighborhood sandwich shop, where you will enjoy some of my all-time favorites with a healthier spin.

BLACKENED BLT FISH PO' BOYS

1 lb (454 g) beef bacon

1 lb (454 g) fresh skinless halibut fillets

1 tbsp (6 g) paprika

1 tbsp (6 g) chili powder

1 tsp garlic powder

½ tsp black pepper

½ tsp ground thyme

½ tsp dried oregano

½ tsp cayenne pepper

1 tsp Creole seasoning

½ tsp onion powder

1 tsp dried basil

½ tsp Himalayan pink salt

4 tbsp (60 ml) olive oil, divided

Light mayonnaise, as needed

3 hoagie buns, toasted

6 leaves romaine lettuce

6 thick slices tomato

When I was a kid, there wasn't a sandwich shop in town that didn't have po' boys on the menu. Filled with anything you could imagine—from sliced roast beef to fried seafood—the only ingredient that remained constant was that crusty-on-the-outside-but-soft-on-the-inside French bread. My version switches things up a bit to create a delicious po' boy centered on grilled blackened halibut. We're going to pass on the fried preparation for this one.

This bacon, lettuce and tomato po' boy starts with a toasted hoagie bun topped with light mayonnaise for added creaminess. Then things go uphill from there. The mild but sweet-tasting fish is then layered—or, as we say in Louisiana, "dressed"—with crispy beef bacon, vibrant romaine lettuce, thick tomato slices and tangy dill pickles. It is one part po' boy, one part BLT—and two parts good!

Preheat the oven to 400°F (204°C). Line a large nonstick baking sheet with parchment paper.

Arrange the beef bacon on the prepared baking sheet. Bake the bacon for 12 to 15 minutes, until it is crispy and some of the fat is rendered.

In the meantime, season both sides of the halibut evenly with the paprika, chili powder, garlic powder, black pepper, thyme, oregano, cayenne pepper, Creole seasoning, onion powder, basil and Himalayan pink salt. Coat the fish lightly with 2 tablespoons (30 ml) of the olive oil.

Heat a 12-inch (30-cm) skillet over medium-high heat, then add the remaining 2 tablespoons (30 ml) of olive oil. Add the halibut fillets and cook them for 4 to 5 minutes on each side, until the meat flakes easily, is opaque in color and reaches an internal temperature of 145°F (63°C).

To serve the sandwiches, spread the mayonnaise on the buns. Layer each sandwich with the halibut, bacon, romaine lettuce and tomatoes.

TENDER PULLED SHORT RIB SANDWICHES

2–3 lb (908 g–1.4 kg) beef short ribs

4 tsp (8 g) Himalayan pink salt, divided

2½ tsp (5 g) smoked paprika, divided

1½ tsp (5 g) garlic powder, divided

2 tsp (4 g) black pepper, divided

3 tbsp (45 ml) olive oil

½ cup (80 g) coarsely chopped white onion

¼ cup (60 ml) Cabernet Sauvignon

3 tsp (6 g) chili powder, divided

2 cups (480 ml) low-sodium beef broth

¾ cup (180 ml) pure maple syrup, divided

2 dried bay leaves

1½ cups (360 ml) tomato puree

½ cup (120 ml) ketchup

¼ cup (60 ml) fresh pineapple juice

2 tbsp (30 ml) Worcestershire sauce

1 tbsp (15 ml) apple cider vinegar

1 tbsp (9 g) minced garlic

1 tsp Sriracha sauce

1 loaf Challah bread

Dill pickle slices, as needed (optional)

If the thought of tender shredded beef sends your taste buds into a frenzy, then this sandwich will be the new thing you crave. And you don't need to wait until your next summer cookout to get things rolling—a quick pressure-cook in your Instant Pot®, and you are halfway there. This decadent sandwich is one for the books: Wine-braised short ribs are tossed in a light, slightly sweet homemade barbecue sauce that is healthier in comparison to a purchased bottle of sauce. Finally, we add a few tart pickles for good measure and serve it on its own. This pulled short rib sandwich will likely become one of your favorites.

Set the Instant Pot to the Sauté setting on high heat.

Season the short ribs evenly with 2 teaspoons (4 g) of the Himalayan pink salt, 1½ teaspoons (3 g) of the smoked paprika, 1 teaspoon of the garlic powder and 1 teaspoon of the black pepper.

Add the olive oil to the Instant Pot, and then sear the short ribs for 2 minutes on each side. Remove the short ribs from the Instant Pot. Add the onion to the Instant Pot and cook it for 5 minutes, stirring occasionally.

Change the Instant Pot's setting to Pressure Cook at high pressure for 45 minutes. Add the Cabernet Sauvignon, 1 teaspoon of the chili powder, 1 teaspoon of Himalayan pink salt, beef broth and ¼ cup (60 ml) of the maple syrup. Stir the mixture for 1 minute. Place the short ribs back into the Instant Pot and top them with the bay leaves. Close and secure the Instant Pot's lid, and then allow it to complete the pressure-cooking process. The Instant Pot will beep once the time is up. Allow for a natural release for 15 minutes, and then do a manual release to finish releasing the pressure. Remove the Instant Pot's lid, then remove the shorts ribs and set them aside.

(continued)

TENDER PULLED SHORT RIB SANDWICHES (CONT.)

While the short ribs are cooking, combine the tomato puree, remaining ½ cup (120 ml) of maple syrup, ketchup, pineapple juice, Worcestershire sauce, apple cider vinegar, minced garlic, remaining 1 teaspoon of Himalayan pink salt, remaining 1 teaspoon of smoked paprika, remaining ½ teaspoon of garlic powder, remaining 1 teaspoon of black pepper, remaining 2 teaspoons (4 g) of chili powder and Sriracha sauce to a 2-quart (1.9-L) saucepan. Bring the sauce to a gentle boil over medium-high heat. Reduce the heat to low, cover the saucepan and cook the sauce for 5 minutes. Once the steam releases from the Instant Pot, remove its lid. Remove the short ribs from the Instant Pot and place them on a large cutting board.

Using two forks, shred the short ribs' meat. Transfer the meat to a large bowl, and then add the barbecue sauce and toss the meat in the sauce to coat it.

To serve the sandwiches, slice the Challah bread in half lengthwise and toast the bread, if desired. Place the shredded barbecue meat on the bread. Top the meat with the dill pickle slices, then slice the bread into four portions and serve the sandwiches.

VEGGIE MUFFULETTA SANDWICHES

2 tbsp (18 g) capers, drained

½ cup (90 g) pitted green olives

½ cup (90 g) pitted Kalamata olives

½ cup (75 g) coarsely chopped roasted red bell peppers

½ cup (80 g) coarsely chopped red onion

¼ cup (25 g) coarsely chopped celery

⅓ cup (30 g) sliced jarred mild banana peppers

2 tbsp plus 1 tsp (21 g) minced garlic

¼ tsp red pepper flakes

1 tsp dried oregano

½ tsp black pepper

⅓ cup plus ¼ cup (140 ml) olive oil, divided

¼ cup (60 ml) red wine vinegar

⅓ cup (80 ml) balsamic vinegar

1 tsp dried basil

4 large portobello mushrooms

1 loaf ciabatta bread

4 slices provolone cheese

If the first thing that comes to mind when you think of a muffuletta is not the tangy, salty and spicy olive relish, then my friends, you have yet to truly experience a muffuletta—that is, until now. This meatless take on a New Orleans classic gets its "meatiness" from rich portobello mushrooms marinated in balsamic vinegar and olive oil. I promise you won't think twice about cured meats and cold cuts.

However, the olive relish steals the show. Bursting with the flavors of olives, capers, roasted red peppers, banana peppers and garlic, the relish just gets better with time. Your sandwich is ready for prime time once your ciabatta bread is toasted, slathered with fresh olive relish and layered with slices of provolone cheese. This is a new kind of good.

In a food processor, combine the capers, green olives, Kalamata olives, red bell peppers, red onion, celery, banana peppers, 2 tablespoons (18 g) of the garlic, red pepper flakes, oregano, black pepper, ¼ cup (60 ml) of the olive oil and red wine vinegar. Pulse two to four times to create a chunky relish. Do not overprocess the ingredients. Transfer the olive relish to a large jar. Cover the jar and refrigerate the relish for at least 8 hours.

In a medium bowl, combine the remaining ⅓ cup (80 ml) of olive oil, balsamic vinegar, basil and remaining 1 teaspoon of garlic. Whisk the ingredients until they form a smooth marinade.

Using a spoon, remove the stems and gills from the portobello mushrooms. Add the portobello mushroom caps to a large bowl. Pour the marinade over the portobello mushrooms. Allow the mushrooms to marinate for 15 minutes.

(continued)

VEGGIE MUFFULETTA SANDWICHES (CONT.)

Meanwhile, preheat the oven to broil. Cut the ciabatta loaf in half lengthwise, then place the bread on a large baking sheet. Toast the bread in the oven for 1 to 2 minutes, or until the bread is lightly browned. Set the bread aside.

Heat a 12-inch (30-cm) skillet over medium heat. Add the mushrooms and cook them for 3 minutes on each side, until the center of each mushroom is tender and the exterior is browned.

Add the olive relish to the bottom half of the ciabatta bread, then top the relish with the mushrooms and provolone cheese.

HEALTHY CHICKEN SLOPPY JOES

1 tbsp (15 ml) olive oil

1 cup (160 g) coarsely chopped white onion

½ cup (75 g) coarsely chopped green bell pepper

3 tbsp (27 g) minced garlic

1 lb (454 g) ground chicken

1 tbsp (16 g) tomato paste

2 tsp (4 g) chili powder

1 tsp black pepper

1 tsp dried oregano

1 tsp paprika

1 tsp Himalayan pink salt

½ tsp garlic powder

¼ tsp red pepper flakes

¼ tsp ground thyme

½ cup (120 ml) tomato puree

1 tsp Worcestershire sauce

1 tsp spicy brown mustard

2 cups (360 g) fire-roasted crushed tomatoes

2 tsp (10 ml) red wine vinegar

½ cup (50 g) grated Parmesan cheese

¼ cup (15 g) finely chopped fresh parsley

6 seeded burger buns, toasted

All hail the sloppy joe—the only meal I could unapologetically eat with my hands. And the messier the sandwich was, the better it was going to be! Growing up, I didn't know a single kid in the South who didn't enjoy a sloppy joe. It was always a quick and easy meal, so my mom never turned down my suggestion.

These sloppy joes, which are made with ground chicken, are a healthy take on the traditional version. The tender chicken simmers in organic tomatoes, Worcestershire sauce and spicy brown mustard combined with garlic, onions and bell pepper for the perfect bite: a little sweet with a bit of heat.

Heat a 10-inch (25-cm) skillet over medium heat. Add the olive oil, onion, bell pepper and minced garlic. Cook the mixture for 10 minutes, stirring it occasionally until the onion is translucent and the bell pepper is soft. Add the chicken, tomato paste, chili powder, black pepper, oregano, paprika, Himalayan pink salt, garlic powder, red pepper flakes and thyme. Stir to combine the ingredients well. Cook the mixture for 5 minutes, stirring it occasionally. Add the tomato puree, Worcestershire sauce, mustard, crushed tomatoes and red wine vinegar. Stir the mixture to combine the ingredients.

Cover the skillet and reduce the heat to medium-low. Cook the sloppy joe filling for 10 minutes. Add the Parmesan cheese and parsley and stir them into the filling.

Serve the sloppy joe filling between the burger buns.

1 medium avocado, pitted
and peeled

½ tbsp (2 g) torn fresh basil
leaves, stems removed

⅓ cup (45 g) pine nuts

2 tbsp (18 g) minced garlic

⅓ cup (80 ml) olive oil

⅔ cup (66 g) grated Parmesan
cheese, divided

1 tsp Himalayan pink salt, divided

1½ tsp (3 g) black pepper, divided

½ tsp ground thyme

1 lb (454 g) lean ground chicken

2 tsp (4 g) dried cilantro

1 tsp dried basil

1 tsp garlic powder

½ tsp ground cumin

½ cup (80 g) finely chopped
white onion

1 large egg

4 slices mozzarella cheese

6 potato burger buns, or 3 potato
burger buns for
double-patty sandwiches

CHICKEN BURGERS WITH AVOCADO PESTO

This recipe will completely change your mind about chicken burgers. Not only is ground chicken a healthier alternative to beef but it's also amazingly versatile and adapts well to so many flavors. This chicken patty is one of the juiciest you'll ever meet, and adding a generous layer of homemade avocado pesto proves that enjoying a better-for-you burger doesn't mean you sacrifice flavor.

Made with heart-healthy avocado, the creamy pesto is decadent without being overly rich and adds a silky texture to the chicken burgers. This burger recipe is as good as it gets. Since this recipe makes six burger patties, feel free to go with one patty or two—because in Texas, we go big or go home.

In a food processor, combine the avocado, fresh basil, pine nuts, minced garlic and olive oil. Process until the ingredients are completely smooth.

Transfer the avocado mixture to a medium bowl. Add ⅓ cup (33 g) of the Parmesan cheese, ½ teaspoon of the Himalayan pink salt, ½ teaspoon of the black pepper and thyme. Whisk the ingredients together until the pesto is smooth, then set it aside.

In a large bowl, combine the chicken, cilantro, dried basil, garlic powder, remaining ½ teaspoon of Himalayan pink salt, remaining 1 teaspoon of black pepper, cumin, onion, egg and remaining ⅓ cup (33 g) of Parmesan cheese. Mix the ingredients well, then form it into six patties.

Heat a 12-inch (30-cm) skillet over medium heat. Cook the chicken patties for 4 minutes on the first side, flip the patties and then add 1 slice of mozzarella cheese to the cooked side. Cook the patties on the opposite side for 4 minutes, until their internal temperature reaches 165°F (74°C) and the center of each patty is firm.

If you prefer six single-patty burgers, place one chicken patty on top of each bottom bun and spread a layer of the avocado pesto on top of the patty, then add the top bun. If you prefer to make three double-patty burgers, place one chicken patty on top of each bottom bun and spread a layer of the avocado pesto on the first patty. Add the second patty and spread another layer of the avocado pesto on top of the second patty. Top the burgers with the top buns and serve them.

JALAPEÑO SLAW

2 cups (178 g) coarsely chopped purple cabbage

½ cup (120 ml) balsamic vinegar

1 tbsp (15 ml) raw unfiltered honey

2 tbsp (30 ml) olive oil

1 tsp lime zest

2 tbsp (30 ml) fresh lime juice

1 tsp minced garlic

½ tsp Himalayan pink salt

¼ tsp ground ginger

¼ cup (23 g) coarsely chopped jalapeño

½ cup (65 g) thinly sliced red onion

¼ cup (4 g) finely chopped fresh cilantro

CHICKEN

1 lb (454 g) boneless, skinless chicken breasts

2 tsp (4 g) paprika

1 tsp Himalayan pink salt

1 tsp black pepper

1 tsp dried cilantro

½ tsp garlic powder

1 tbsp (15 ml) olive oil

4 whole wheat burger buns

Light mayonnaise (optional)

LOW-FAT CHICKEN BREAST SANDWICHES WITH JALAPEÑO SLAW

Grilled chicken sandwiches are not dull anymore, especially after giving them an upgrade with a tangy, sweet and slightly spicy jalapeño coleslaw!

First, tender chicken breasts are butterflied, tenderized and seasoned. Then they are grilled to perfection. They are complemented by a vibrant combination of fresh purple cabbage and a slew of Tex-Mex flavors. And because a bit of a kick is always a welcomed treat, we can't forget about the jalapeño. Did I mention the slaw is sugar-free?

This bold and fresh take on a chicken breast sandwich is perfect for summer cookouts and barbecues!

To make the jalapeño slaw, combine the purple cabbage, balsamic vinegar, honey, olive oil, lime zest, lime juice, minced garlic, Himalayan pink salt, ginger, jalapeño, onion and cilantro in a medium bowl. Mix the ingredients together well, then transfer them to a large jar. Secure the jar's lid, then gently shake the jar to further combine the ingredients. Place the jar in the refrigerator and allow the slaw to marinate for at least 2 hours.

To make the chicken, butterfly each of the chicken breasts into two thin slices. Cover the chicken with plastic wrap and pound the chicken using a meat tenderizer until the meat is ½ inch (1.3 cm) thick. Season the chicken breast evenly on both sides with the paprika, Himalayan pink salt, black pepper, cilantro and garlic powder.

Heat a 12-inch (30-cm) skillet over medium-high heat, and then add the olive oil. Add the chicken and cook it for 3 to 4 minutes on each side, until the meat's juices run clear and the meat is opaque throughout.

To serve the sandwiches, layer a bottom bun with light mayonnaise (if using), place a chicken breast on a burger bun and top the chicken with a generous serving of the jalapeño slaw before topping the sandwich with the other half of the burger bun.

CREOLE-SPICED LAMB BURGERS

Lamb burgers are one of my favorites. They are so flavorful that they can stand alone with minimal effort. So, when I wanted to create something new, going back to my roots was a perfect idea.

For this recipe, I paired the lamb with traditional flavors you would typically associate with lamb—like fresh rosemary—but the Creole seasoning brings the additional flavors of oregano, bay leaf, basil, thyme, parsley and paprika. The herbs, spices, egg and Parmesan cheese are folded into the meat to ensure that the flavors run deep and the meat is extra juicy. Not only is this lamb delicious, but it has tons of good stuff like protein, iron, zinc and vitamin B12.

1 lb (454 g) ground lamb

2 tsp (2 g) finely chopped fresh rosemary

1 tsp dried oregano

1 tsp dried parsley

1 tsp dried basil

1 tsp Creole seasoning

½ tsp garlic powder

1 tsp black pepper

½ tsp Himalayan pink salt

⅛ tsp cayenne pepper

¼ cup (40 g) finely chopped onion

1 tbsp (6 g) finely chopped jalapeño

1 tsp minced garlic

1 tsp hot sauce

1 large egg

⅓ cup (33 g) grated Parmesan cheese

4 slices pepper Jack cheese

4 brioche burger buns

Romaine lettuce (optional)

Sliced pickled jalapeños (optional)

In a large bowl, combine the lamb, rosemary, oregano, parsley, basil, Creole seasoning, garlic powder, black pepper, Himalayan pink salt, cayenne pepper, onion, jalapeño, minced garlic, hot sauce, egg and Parmesan cheese. Mix the ingredients until they are combined. Form the lamb mixture into four patties.

Heat a 12-inch (30-cm) skillet over medium heat. Add the patties and cook them for 4 to 5 minutes on the first side. Flip the burgers, top each one with a slice of the pepper Jack cheese and cook the second side for 4 to 5 minutes, until the internal temperature of the patties reaches 165°F (74°C).

To serve the burgers, add the lettuce (if using) to a burger bun, then layer with a lamb patty and top each patty with the sliced pickled jalapeños (if using).

BISON SLIDERS WITH CARAMELIZED ONIONS

1 tbsp (14 g) unsalted butter

3 tbsp (56 g) coconut oil

1 cup (130 g) thinly sliced white onion

4 tbsp (60 ml) red wine, divided

1 tbsp (15 ml) water

¼ tsp baking powder

1⅛ tsp (2 g) Himalayan pink salt, divided

1 lb (454 g) ground bison

1 tsp ground thyme

1 tsp white pepper

1 tsp paprika

½ tsp dried oregano

¼ cup (25 g) grated Parmesan cheese

1 tbsp (1 g) finely chopped fresh cilantro

1 large egg

Strawberry-pepper jam, as needed (optional)

8 slider buns

Baby arugula, as needed (optional)

When I have burgers on the brain but I want to go lean, I reach for this bison burger recipe. Bison burgers pack much less saturated fat than your typical ground beef burger patties.

Prepared in slider form, rich and hearty bison patties are grilled and served simply with wine-soaked caramelized onions and optional fresh baby arugula. And since sliders are always a hit, these bison burger sliders are a game changer for any crowd. If this is your first time venturing into the world of wild game, I think you'll be pleasantly surprised. Don't hesitate; just dive right in.

Heat a 10-inch (25-cm) skillet over medium-high heat. Add the butter, coconut oil and onion to the skillet. Cook the onion for 3 to 5 minutes, stirring it occasionally, then add 2 tablespoons (30 ml) of the red wine. Cook the onion for another 5 minutes. Add the water and baking powder. Cook the onion for another 10 minutes, then add the remaining 2 tablespoons (30 ml) of red wine and ⅛ teaspoon of the Himalayan pink salt. Cook the onion for another 10 minutes, stirring it occasionally, until the onion is reddish-brown in color and translucent. Remove the skillet from the heat.

Add the bison to a large bowl. Season the meat evenly with the thyme, white pepper, paprika, oregano and remaining 1 teaspoon of Himalayan pink salt. Add the Parmesan cheese, cilantro and egg. Mix the ingredients together well. Form the bison mixture into eight slider-sized patties.

Heat a 12-inch (30-cm) skillet over medium heat. Add the patties and cook them for 3 to 5 minutes on each side, until their juices run clear and their internal temperature reaches 160°F (71°C).

To serve the burgers, spread the strawberry-pepper jam (if using) on the bottom slider buns, then place the bison patties on the strawberry jam before topping the patties with the caramelized onion and arugula (if using).

LOW-FAT CHICKEN SALAD SANDWICHES

1 lb (454 g) boneless, skinless chicken breasts, cut into small cubes

1 tsp Himalayan pink salt, divided

1 tsp black pepper, divided

¾ tsp garlic powder, divided

1 tbsp (15 ml) olive oil

¼ cup (60 ml) light mayonnaise

¼ cup (60 ml) crème fraîche

2 tsp (6 g) minced garlic

½ cup (80 g) coarsely chopped red onion

1 tsp fresh lemon juice

1 tsp spicy brown mustard

1 tsp dried basil

½ cup (76 g) purple grapes, cut in half

¼ tsp celery salt

¼ tsp ground turmeric

⅛ tsp cayenne pepper

4 croissants, sliced and toasted

4 leaves romaine lettuce

A handful of fresh ingredients, along with a slew of seasoning and spices, are transformed into light, cold, creamy chicken salad sandwiches. I've enjoyed my fair share of chicken salad recipes over the years, and striking the perfect balance is key. The consistency of this chicken salad is spot-on. It's far from being dry, yet it's not overly creamy, and I use a combination of crème fraîche and light mayonnaise to shave off some calories and fat. Chunky pieces of tender chicken breast, slightly crunchy red onion and sweet purple grapes all add to the flavor and texture of the salad. Serve your chicken salad on a toasted, buttery croissant or in lettuce wraps.

Season the chicken pieces evenly with ½ teaspoon of the Himalayan pink salt, ½ teaspoon of the black pepper and ½ teaspoon of the garlic powder.

Heat a 12-inch (30-cm) skillet over medium-high heat, and then add the olive oil and chicken. Cook the chicken for 6 to 8 minutes, stirring it often, until the meat is opaque throughout.

Transfer the chicken to a large bowl and allow it to cool completely. Add the mayonnaise, crème fraîche, minced garlic, red onion, lemon juice, brown mustard, basil, grapes, celery salt, turmeric, cayenne pepper, remaining ½ teaspoon of Himalayan pink salt, remaining ½ teaspoon of black pepper and remaining ¼ teaspoon of garlic powder. Mix the ingredients until they are well combined.

To serve the sandwiches, put the chicken salad in the croissants and then top the chicken salad with a leaf of romaine lettuce. Alternatively, omit the croissants and serve the chicken salad wrapped in the romaine lettuce.

TURKEY MEATBALL SUBS

My family loves meatballs, and while meatballs are great on their own, something magical happens when you place them in buttery brioche buns. But the most magical part of this recipe is the turkey meatballs themselves. With the inclusion of a few unique ingredients to make them super tender, you may never go back to beef meatballs. Plus, turkey is much lower in saturated fat, making this a healthier take on the traditional.

1 lb (454 g) lean ground turkey

1 tsp paprika

1½ tsp (3 g) black pepper, divided

1 tsp garlic powder, divided

½ tsp dried oregano

¾ tsp Himalayan pink salt, divided

2 tbsp (4 g) finely chopped fresh basil, divided

⅓ cup (33 g) grated Parmesan cheese

1 large egg

2 cups (480 ml) tomato sauce

¼ tsp red pepper flakes

6 brioche hot dog buns

6 slices provolone cheese

Preheat the oven to 350°F (177°C). Lightly grease a medium nonstick baking sheet.

In a large bowl, combine the turkey, paprika, 1 teaspoon of the black pepper, ½ teaspoon of the garlic powder, oregano, ½ teaspoon of the Himalayan pink salt, 1 tablespoon (2 g) of the basil, Parmesan cheese and egg. Mix the ingredients together well, then form the meat mixture into golf ball–sized meatballs. Place the meatballs on the prepared baking sheet. Bake the meatballs for 15 minutes, until their internal temperature reaches 165°F (74°C).

Meanwhile, in a 2-quart (1.9-L) saucepan over low heat, combine the tomato sauce, red pepper flakes, remaining ½ teaspoon of black pepper, remaining ½ teaspoon of garlic powder, remaining ¼ teaspoon of Himalayan pink salt and remaining 1 tablespoon (2 g) of basil. Cook the mixture for 5 minutes.

Once the turkey meatballs are done baking, transfer them to a large bowl. Top the meatballs with the seasoned tomato sauce, then gently toss the meatballs to coat them with the sauce.

Preheat the oven to broil. Meanwhile, place the baked meatballs on the hot dog buns and add additional tomato sauce. Top each sub with the provolone cheese and place the sandwiches on a large baking sheet. Broil the subs for 1 to 2 minutes, or until the cheese melts.

WHOLESOME SOUPS
TO WARM YOUR SOUL

If we didn't have anything else in the house, we always had soup, and hence my love for soups came to be. Soups will keep you warm on those cold winter days and are just as satisfying as any other meal. Even though I grew up eating soups from the can, I also enjoyed many incredible soups and stews made from scratch. I have fond memories of walking into the house and smelling the aromas of homemade beef stew or chicken noodle soup on the stove. And if someone got sick, it was almost guaranteed that soup was on the way.

The rich, robust and limitless flavors of soups and stews were so good and hearty that as a kid, I never thought I was eating healthy. Experiencing the love and effort behind those meals, I learned to appreciate the result before it was all gone. Throughout my years of preparing soups and experiencing cultures outside of my own, I started to realize how versatile their textures and flavors could be. Being able to appreciate different cultures outside of the South was an eye-opening experience. Whether it was a creamy sweet potato and zucchini soup in Mexico or a truffled asparagus soup in Napa Valley, soups and stews lit up my creativity.

In this chapter, you'll be pleasantly surprised to find family favorites, like my Healthier Baked Potato Soup (page 81), which is super flavorful. It's topped off with bits of beef bacon, shredded Cheddar cheese and crème fraîche to give you all the vibes of a fully loaded baked potato. If you love tomato soups, then my smooth Silky Roasted-Tomato Bisque (page 78) will light up your taste buds. The nutty flavor from the Parmesan cheese paired with garlic and herbs will have you feeling nice and cozy from the inside out. And I'd be remiss if I didn't mention the Five-Star Truffled Mushroom Cream Soup (page 82). This soup is slightly textured from the freshly pureed mushrooms, and the aroma from the truffle is intoxicating. Finally, you will also get to experience a creation that I feel represents my heritage. My Low-Sodium Pontchartrain Stew (page 74) screams, "Welcome to the Louisiana bayou"—with a kick! This chapter will showcase my transition from eating canned soups to creating some of the tastiest and better-for-you soups from scratch.

LOW-SODIUM PONTCHARTRAIN STEW

2 lb (908 g) fresh skinless cod loin fillets, cut into medium cubes

3 tsp (6 g) Creole seasoning, divided

2 tsp (4 g) black pepper, divided

2½ tsp (5 g) dried oregano, divided

1½ tsp (5 g) garlic powder, divided

½ cup (80 g) coarsely chopped onion

¼ cup (25 g) coarsely chopped celery

½ cup (75 g) coarsely chopped green bell pepper

¼ cup (57 g) unsalted butter

3 tbsp (27 g) minced garlic

¼ cup (60 ml) white wine

1 cup (240 ml) low-sodium chicken stock

½ cup (120 ml) low-fat condensed cream of mushroom soup

1 tbsp (15 ml) hot sauce

1½ cups (360 ml) canned light coconut milk

½ cup (50 g) grated Parmesan cheese

1 tbsp (8 g) all-purpose flour

½ tsp red pepper flakes

½ tsp dried basil

¼ tsp cayenne pepper

¼ tsp rubbed sage

There's just something about buttery cod blended with a rich and creamy sauce that makes you want to make this soupy stew over and over again! The key to this recipe is the coconut milk, which creates an amazing consistency and sets the tone for the fresh fish to absorb all of the delicious flavors around it—and it's much lighter than using heavy cream. Last but not least, the cod is flavorful, low in mercury and has a wonderfully delicate texture. This dish is a win-win for flavor and health.

It doesn't matter if it's a hot Texas day or a not-so-frequent freezing Texas night; this fish stew is one of my favorites. It's what comes to mind when I think of home and has Louisiana written all over it. The soup's richness paired with generous chunks of savory cod and well-balanced seasonings make this soup perfect as a starter or served solo with a bed of brown rice.

Season the cod pieces evenly with 1 teaspoon of the Creole seasoning, 1 teaspoon of the black pepper, ½ teaspoon of the oregano and ½ teaspoon of the garlic powder. Set the cod aside.

In a food processor, combine the onion, celery and bell pepper. Pulse five to seven times, until the vegetables are finely chopped. Set the vegetables aside.

Heat a 5-quart (4.8-L) sauté pan over medium heat, and then add the butter and minced garlic. Cook the garlic for 2 minutes, stirring it occasionally. Add the onion, celery and bell pepper and cook the mixture for 5 minutes, stirring it occasionally, or until the onion becomes translucent. Add the white wine and chicken stock. Cook the mixture for 2 minutes, stirring it occasionally.

Add the cream of mushroom soup, hot sauce, coconut milk and Parmesan cheese and stir to combine the ingredients. Add the flour, remaining 2 teaspoons (4 g) of Creole seasoning, remaining 1 teaspoon of black pepper, remaining 2 teaspoons (4 g) of oregano, remaining 1 teaspoon of garlic powder, red pepper flakes, basil, cayenne pepper and sage. Stir to combine the ingredients, and then fold in the cod. Cover the sauté pan and cook the stew for 10 minutes, until the cod is opaque throughout.

CREAMY CORN CHOWDER

Easy to pull together, this mouthwatering corn chowder is a simple blend of fresh and naturally sweet white corn, onions, vegetable broth and seasonings. And to turn these fresh ingredients into a truly hearty, thick chowder, I add Parmesan cheese and 2 percent milk. This recipe proves that you can make some of the creamiest soups without a single drop of heavy cream in sight.

1 tbsp (14 g) unsalted butter

2 tbsp (30 ml) olive oil

2 tbsp (18 g) minced garlic

½ cup (80 g) coarsely chopped red onion

½ cup (25 g) coarsely chopped green onion

2 tbsp (16 g) arrowroot flour

3 cups (462 g) fresh sweet white corn kernels

2 tsp (4 g) smoked paprika

1 tsp white pepper

1 tsp Himalayan pink salt

1 tsp garlic powder

½ tsp ground allspice

¼ tsp ground cumin

3 cups (720 ml) low-sodium vegetable broth

1 cup (240 ml) 2% milk

¼ cup (25 g) grated Parmesan cheese

Heat a 4-quart (3.8-L) saucepan over medium heat. Add the butter and olive oil, and allow the butter to melt. Add the minced garlic and cook it for 1 minute. Add the red onion and green onion. Cook the mixture for 5 minutes, stirring it occasionally, then add the arrowroot flour. Cook the mixture for 1 to 2 minutes, stirring it frequently until a thick paste forms.

Add the corn, smoked paprika, white pepper, Himalayan pink salt, garlic powder, allspice and cumin to the onion and garlic mixture. Cook the corn for 3 to 4 minutes. Add the vegetable broth and bring the mixture to a gentle boil. Cover the saucepan, reduce the heat to medium-low and cook the mixture for 10 minutes.

Uncover the saucepan and allow the mixture to cool for 10 minutes. It is important to allow the mixture to cool slightly before blending it. Hot liquids may splatter out of the blender if they are not covered properly with a lid.

Transfer the mixture to a blender. Blend the mixture for 1 to 2 minutes, until it is smooth. Pour the blended mixture back into the saucepan, then add the milk and Parmesan cheese. Stir the chowder until it is smooth, then serve it.

SILKY ROASTED-TOMATO BISQUE

My first introduction to tomato bisque was quite interesting. The bisque was paired with a grilled cheese sandwich, and I honestly didn't know whether to dip the sandwich into the soup or eat first one and then the other. I clearly put way too much thought into the process. A few minutes in, I was focused entirely on the bisque—it was way different from the salty canned tomato soup I'd had as a kid.

Tomatoes, low-sodium vegetable stock, herbs, onions and a hint of agave nectar are simmered before being blended. And the coconut milk makes this bisque velvety, rich and better for you. It's the savory comfort food you need on a chilly day.

1 tbsp (15 ml) olive oil

⅓ cup (30 g) coarsely chopped leek

1 cup (160 g) coarsely chopped red onion

1 tbsp (9 g) minced garlic

3 tbsp (48 g) tomato paste

2 cups (360 g) crushed tomatoes

2 cups (360 g) fire-roasted diced tomatoes

2 tsp (4 g) dried oregano

2 tsp (4 g) Himalayan pink salt

1 tsp black pepper

1 tsp garlic powder

¼ tsp ground turmeric

¼ tsp cayenne pepper

4 cups (960 ml) low-sodium vegetable stock

1 tsp fresh thyme leaves

1 tsp light agave nectar

1½ cups (360 ml) canned light coconut milk

1 cup (100 g) grated Parmesan cheese

Heat a 4-quart (3.8-L) saucepan over medium heat. Add the olive oil, leek, red onion and minced garlic. Cook the mixture for 5 minutes, stirring it occasionally. Add the tomato paste, crushed tomatoes, diced tomatoes, oregano, Himalayan pink salt, black pepper, garlic powder, turmeric, cayenne pepper, vegetable broth, thyme and agave nectar. Stir the ingredients to combine them well. Cover the saucepan, reduce the heat to medium-low and cook the mixture for 10 minutes.

Uncover the saucepan and allow the mixture to cool for 10 minutes. It is important to allow the mixture to cool slightly before blending it. Hot liquids may splatter out of the blender if they are not covered properly with a lid.

Transfer the mixture to a blender and blend it for 1 to 2 minutes, until it is smooth.

Strain the soup into a large bowl using a mesh strainer, slightly pressing the ingredients through the mesh with the back of a large spoon. Transfer the strained soup to the saucepan and set it over medium-low heat. Bring the soup to a simmer, then add the coconut milk and the Parmesan cheese. Stir the soup until it is completely smooth, then remove it from the heat and serve it.

HEALTHIER BAKED POTATO SOUP

2 tbsp (28 g) unsalted butter

2 tbsp (18 g) minced garlic

1 lb (454 g) red potatoes, quartered

2½ tsp (5 g) Himalayan pink salt

1 tsp black pepper

1 tsp garlic powder

¼ tsp ground ginger

3 cups (720 ml) low-sodium chicken stock

½ cup (120 ml) crème fraîche

1 cup (240 ml) canned light coconut milk

1 cup (100 g) grated Parmesan cheese

1 tbsp (3 g) finely chopped fresh chives

2 strips beef bacon

¼ cup (28 g) shredded sharp Cheddar cheese

If you could turn your loaded baked potato into a soup, this is precisely what you would get! The only difference is that I've swapped a few heavy ingredients for lighter versions. Traditional baked potato soup is notorious for being loaded with calories, but you'll find this recipe gives you all the things you crave with less guilt, yet it's still hearty and filling.

It all starts with red potatoes, which gives the soup its subtly sweet flavor and smooth texture instead of the starchy consistency you get from russet potatoes. Coconut milk, low-sodium chicken stock and crème fraîche join the show, and that's when things really get going. The tasty yet optional finale is the sharp Cheddar cheese and beef bacon on top. Who wants to sign up?

Heat a 4-quart (3.8-L) saucepan over medium heat. Add the butter and minced garlic, stirring the mixture until the butter melts. Add the potatoes, then season them evenly with the Himalayan pink salt, black pepper, garlic powder and ginger. Cook the mixture for 5 minutes, stirring it occasionally. Add the chicken stock, cover the saucepan and cook the mixture for 20 minutes, or until the potatoes are tender.

Uncover the saucepan and allow the mixture to cool for 10 minutes. It is important to allow the mixture to cool slightly before blending it. Hot liquids may splatter out of the blender if they are not covered properly with a lid.

Transfer the mixture to a blender and blend it for 1 to 2 minutes, until it is completely smooth.

Pour the blended mixture into the saucepan, then add the crème fraîche, coconut milk, Parmesan cheese and chives. Stir the ingredients together until the soup is smooth.

Preheat the oven to 400°F (204°C). Place the beef bacon strips in the oven for 12 minutes at. Then remove from the oven and chop into small pieces.

To serve the soup, ladle the soup into bowls and top each serving with the Cheddar cheese and bacon.

FIVE-STAR TRUFFLED MUSHROOM CREAM SOUP

1 tbsp (15 ml) olive oil

2 tbsp (18 g) minced garlic

½ cup (80 g) coarsely chopped white onion

4 cups (280 g) presliced cremini mushrooms

1 tsp garlic powder

1 tsp rubbed sage

1 tsp black pepper

½ tsp ground allspice

½ tsp ground thyme

1 tsp Himalayan pink salt

¼ tsp dried tarragon

3 cups (720 ml) low-sodium vegetable broth

¾ cup (170 g) Urbani Truffle Thrills (White Truffles and Porcini flavor)

1 tbsp (15 ml) white truffle oil

3 tbsp (45 ml) cashew milk

1 cup (240 ml) canned light coconut milk

This mushroom soup is the epitome of the food I grew up enjoying and the recipes I love to create. It's no secret I am a fan of mushrooms—of any variety. And did someone say Urbani Truffle Thrills? Easily found online or at your local Italian grocer, this creamy combination of truffle and mushrooms is another ingredient I had no clue existed until I was fully grown. And now that I am in the know, I use it when I want to take things up a notch. It's my secret ingredient.

Although this soup uses coconut milk and cashew milk in place of heavy cream, it doesn't lose any of the creamy texture you would expect. The savory mushrooms are the perfect accompaniment to balance the various seasonings, and the truffle oil is subtle and doesn't overpower anything in its path. If you're looking for an elegant starter that tastes as though you're enjoying a five-star dining experience, then this is the soup for you!

Heat a 4-quart (3.8-L) saucepan over medium heat. Add the olive oil and minced garlic, and cook it for 1 minute. Add the onion. Cook the onion for 5 minutes, stirring it occasionally. Add the mushrooms, garlic powder, sage, black pepper, allspice, thyme, Himalayan pink salt and tarragon. Cook the mixture for 5 minutes, stirring it occasionally.

Add the vegetable broth and bring the mixture to a gentle boil. Cover the saucepan, reduce the heat to medium-low and cook the mixture for 10 minutes.

Uncover the saucepan and allow the mixture to cool for 10 minutes. It is important to allow the mixture to cool slightly before blending it. Hot liquids may splatter out of the blender if they are not covered properly with a lid.

Transfer the mixture to a blender. Blend the mixture for 1 to 2 minutes, until it is completely smooth.

Transfer the soup to the saucepan, and then set the saucepan over low heat. Add the truffle thrills, truffle oil, cashew milk and coconut milk. Stir the ingredients together until the soup is smooth, cover the saucepan and cook the soup for 5 minutes, until it is heated through. Serve the soup immediately.

A LIGHTER SOMETHING
TO HOLD YOU OVER

When dining out, I always look forward to the appetizers. For one, they minimize the time between me and my main course! Even when I have family and friends over for a game night, having bite-sized finger foods to snack on holds them over while they await the main dish. Even as a kid, I was introduced to the hors d'oeuvre. Whether it was snacking on freshly sliced tomatoes before our evening meal or grabbing a handful of pickled cucumbers or fried okra—small bites kept us from getting too hungry before dinnertime. I guess I've always been a lover of predinner meals before I even knew they were called appetizers.

Now that you've landed in the appetizer chapter, I'll be sharing a few of my creations that are based on the things I learned and enjoyed about those predinner meals as a kid. Here you'll find healthier versions of some tasty appetizers from my roots in southern Louisiana and beyond.

What do you have to look forward to in this chapter? How about my Oxtails and Potato Croquettes with Sage-Butter Sauce (page 86)? It will knock your socks off and awaken your senses from smell to taste. If you're a lover of mushrooms, my Garlic and Parmesan Stuffed Mushrooms (page 109), filled with herbs and Parmesan cheese, are great starters for any occasion. And I think it's safe to say most people are fans of deviled eggs. My Creole-Style Salmon Deviled Eggs (page 95) are perfectly balanced, with slightly smoky Cajun flavors and chunks of moist and flavorful salmon.

Daddy Paul was a heavy influence in the sweet potato department, and my Fully Loaded Baked Sweet Potato Fries (page 89) will be a pleasant surprise. Fire-roasted poblano pepper, vibrant avocado, earthy black beans, crumbled queso fresco cheese and a spicy homemade cilantro aioli make this a home run and just may replace your typical loaded cheesy fries. And because wings are a staple for any gathering, I wanted to bring something a little different to the table. My Honey, Lemon and Parmesan Baked Chicken Wings (page 105) are free of refined sugar and are pleasantly herbaceous. The light glaze that coats these wings will raise an eyebrow or two. So sit back and enjoy "A Lighter Something to Hold You Over" anytime and without the guilt.

OXTAILS AND POTATO CROQUETTES WITH SAGE-BUTTER SAUCE

OXTAILS

3 lb (1.4 kg) beef oxtails

2 tsp (4 g) Himalayan pink salt, divided

2 tsp (4 g) black pepper, divided

1½ tsp (5 g) garlic powder, divided

1 tsp ground thyme, divided

¼ tsp ground ginger

2 tbsp (30 ml) olive oil

1½ cups (360 ml) Pinot Noir wine

2¼ cups (600 ml) low-sodium beef stock

2 tbsp (30 ml) Worcestershire sauce

1 tbsp (9 g) minced garlic

1 tsp onion powder

1 sprig fresh rosemary

½ cup (50 g) grated Parmesan cheese

When you really want to impress, you must turn to this recipe. Created by combining two recipes, this appetizer is as southern as you can get in a single, decadent bite.

Now close your eyes and imagine this—seasoned red potatoes are blended with cheese and rolled in a light panko breading to make the best crispy potato croquettes you've ever had. And because the croquettes are baked, the cholesterol is reduced and so is the amount of fat. Next, oxtails are braised in red wine, pressure-cooked to ensure tenderness, shredded and placed on each croquette. Time is taken to separate the meat from the fat, ensuring you only get the good stuff and none of the bad. Finally, a light sage-butter sauce is drizzled over both the oxtail and potato croquettes, lifting the flavors even more. And before you take your first bite, a light sprinkle of grated Parmesan cheese is added for more sharpness.

Serving this dish as an appetizer allows you to enjoy a decadent dish in a smaller, more approachable portion. If that's not a one-bite wonder, then I don't know what is.

To make the oxtails, turn the Instant Pot to the Sauté setting on high heat. Season the oxtails with 1 teaspoon of the Himalayan pink salt, 1 teaspoon of the black pepper, 1 teaspoon of the garlic powder, ½ teaspoon of the thyme and ginger. Add the olive oil to the Instant Pot, and then sear the oxtails for 2 minutes on each side. Remove the oxtails from the Instant Pot and set them aside.

Change the Instant Pot's setting to Pressure Cook at high pressure for 45 minutes. In the pot, combine the Pinot Noir wine, beef stock, Worcestershire sauce, minced garlic, onion powder, remaining 1 teaspoon of Himalayan pink salt, remaining 1 teaspoon of black pepper, remaining ½ teaspoon of garlic powder and the remaining ½ teaspoon of thyme. Stir the ingredients to combine them thoroughly. Place the oxtails in the Instant Pot and place the rosemary on top of them. Close and secure the Instant Pot's lid and allow the oxtails to pressure cook.

(continued)

POTATO CROQUETTES

2 lb (908 g) red potatoes

1½ cups (150 g) grated Parmesan cheese, divided

½ cup (57 g) shredded sharp Cheddar cheese

1 large egg

2 tsp (4 g) dried basil

1 tsp Himalayan pink salt

1 tsp black pepper

½ tsp onion powder

1 cup (56 g) panko breadcrumbs

SAGE-BUTTER SAUCE

¼ cup (57 g) unsalted butter

¼ cup (60 ml) olive oil

10 whole fresh sage leaves

1 tbsp (9 g) minced garlic

1 tbsp (2 g) dried parsley

OXTAILS AND POTATO CROQUETTES WITH SAGE-BUTTER SAUCE (CONT.)

While the oxtails are cooking, prepare the potato croquettes. Peel and quarter the red potatoes. Place the potatoes in a large pot and fill it with cold water, making sure the potatoes are fully submerged. Set the pot over high heat and bring the water to a boil. Cook the potatoes for 25 minutes, or until they are tender. Drain the potatoes and transfer them to a large bowl. Mash the potatoes using a potato masher, then add 1 cup (100 g) of Parmesan cheese, Cheddar cheese, egg, basil, Himalayan pink salt, black pepper and onion powder. Mix the ingredients together thoroughly with a large fork or spatula. Allow the mixture to cool completely.

Preheat the oven to 400°F (204°C). Line a large nonstick baking sheet with parchment paper.

Using your hand or a 3-inch (8-cm) round cookie cutter, form the potato mixture into croquettes. With your thumb, make a small indentation in the top of each croquette. In a medium bowl, combine the panko breadcrumbs and remaining ½ cup (50 g) of the Parmesan cheese, then toss the potato croquettes in the breadcrumb mixture until they are coated. Place the potato croquettes on the prepared baking sheet and bake them for 20 to 25 minutes, until they are golden brown.

To make the sage-butter sauce, heat a 2-quart (1.9-L) saucepan over medium heat. Add the butter and olive oil. When the butter begins to foam, add the sage leaves, minced garlic and parsley. Cook the sauce for 4 to 6 minutes, until the butter has completely melted and the sauce is fragrant. Remove and discard the sage leaves.

Once the Instant Pot's timer has beeped, allow the pressure to release naturally for 15 minutes, then manually release the remaining pressure. Open the Instant Pot's lid and remove the oxtails. Transfer them to a large cutting board. Separate the meat from the bones and shred the meat using a fork.

To serve, top each potato croquette with a portion of the shredded oxtail, followed by the sage-butter sauce and the Parmesan cheese.

FULLY LOADED BAKED SWEET POTATO FRIES

1 large sweet potato, peeled

¾ tsp Himalayan pink salt, divided

¾ tsp black pepper, divided

½ tsp smoked paprika

¼ tsp ground cinnamon

¼ tsp ground turmeric

¼ cup plus 1 tbsp (75 ml) olive oil

1 cup (172 g) black beans, drained and rinsed

1 tsp minced garlic

¾ tsp garlic powder, divided

1 large poblano pepper

½ cup (120 ml) light mayonnaise

2 tbsp (30 ml) hot sauce

1 tbsp (15 ml) fresh lemon juice

2 tsp (4 g) dried cilantro

¼ tsp ground ginger

¼ tsp cayenne pepper

1 medium avocado

¼ cup (38 g) crumbled queso fresco cheese

Fresh cilantro leaves, as needed

Doesn't the word "loaded" make you want to jump right into this recipe? I don't know about you, but when I see a recipe is loaded, I know it's filled with all the good things—which I'm always game for. Well, if you have your mouth ready for some lightened-up deliciousness, say hello to these loaded baked sweet potato fries.

Traditionally, loaded fries are not what we would consider nutritious. But when you use sweet potatoes, you bump up the vitamins and fiber for a very tasty and satisfying snack that is perfect for sharing. I bake the sweet potatoes, then top them with roasted and chopped poblano peppers, black beans, chunks of fresh avocado and a sprinkle of crumbly queso fresco cheese for even more flavor. And for the obligatory drool moment, spicy cilantro aioli closes the show. Trust me on this—you're going to love these!

Preheat the oven to 400°F (204°C). Lightly grease a large nonstick baking sheet.

Chop the sweet potato into fries that are 3 inches (8 cm) long and ½ inch (1.3 cm) wide. Place the sweet potato fries in a large bowl. Add ½ teaspoon of the Himalayan pink salt, ½ teaspoon of the black pepper, smoked paprika, cinnamon and turmeric and toss the fries to season them with the spices. Pour ¼ cup (60 ml) of the olive oil evenly over the sweet potatoes, then toss the fries until they are evenly coated with oil. Spread out the sweet potato fries on the prepared baking sheet and bake them for 10 minutes. Gently flip the sweet potato fries and bake them for 10 minutes, until they are tender inside and browned along the edges.

While the sweet potato fries are baking, combine the black beans, minced garlic and ½ teaspoon of the garlic powder in a 2-quart (1.9-L) saucepan over low heat and cook the beans for 5 to 7 minutes, until the beans are hot. Set the beans aside.

(continued)

FULLY LOADED BAKED SWEET POTATO FRIES (CONT.)

Place the poblano pepper directly over an open flame and roast it for 3 to 4 minutes on each side, until the skin is charred. To roast the poblano in the oven instead, preheat the oven to 400°F (204°C). Lightly grease a medium nonstick baking sheet. Place the poblano on the prepared baking sheet and roast the poblano for 20 to 30 minutes, flipping it occasionally, until its skin is charred. Remove the poblano from the oven.

Transfer the charred poblano to a medium bowl and cover it. Allow the poblano to steam in the bowl for 10 minutes to loosen the skin. Once the poblano is cool enough to handle, remove and discard the skin, stem and seeds. Chop the poblano into small pieces.

In a small bowl, combine the mayonnaise, hot sauce, lemon juice, remaining 1 tablespoon (15 ml) of olive oil, dried cilantro, ginger, cayenne pepper, remaining ¼ teaspoon of Himalayan pink salt, remaining ¼ teaspoon of black pepper and remaining ¼ teaspoon of garlic powder. Whisk until the aioli is smooth.

Peel the avocado, remove the pit and cut half of the avocado into small chunks. You can use the remaining avocado as an extra topping or in another dish later.

To serve, top the sweet potato fries with the black beans, poblano pepper and avocado. Finally, top the fries with the queso fresco cheese and a drizzle of cilantro aioli. Garnish the fries with the fresh cilantro leaves.

FLAMING HOT JALAPEÑO POPPERS

1 large poblano pepper

6 to 8 large jalapeños

1 cup (224 g) Neufchâtel cheese

1 cup (113 g) shredded sharp Cheddar cheese

⅓ cup (33 g) grated Parmesan cheese

1 tbsp (9 g) minced garlic

1 tsp chili powder

1 tsp smoked paprika

½ tsp garlic powder

½ tsp Himalayan pink salt

½ tsp black pepper

¼ tsp red pepper flakes

¼ tsp cayenne pepper

½ cup (28 g) panko breadcrumbs

1 tbsp (15 ml) olive oil

These vibrant jalapeños are filled with three different cheeses and roasted poblano peppers and topped with crispy baked panko bread-crumbs.

To make this dish a little healthier, I substitute the usual cream cheese with Neufchâtel cheese. In addition to having a higher moisture content, which makes the filling extra creamy, Neufchâtel cheese is like cream cheese in both flavor and texture but contains less fat. Feel free to "pop" your poppers solo style or dip them in a light ranch dressing for an additional wow factor.

Roast the poblano pepper over the open flame of a gas stove or grill for 3 to 4 minutes on each side, until its skin is charred. To roast the poblano pepper in the oven instead, preheat the oven to 400°F (204°C). Lightly grease a medium nonstick baking sheet. Place the whole poblano on the prepared baking sheet. Bake the poblano for 20 to 30 minutes, flipping it occasionally, until its skin is charred. Remove the poblano from the oven.

Transfer the charred poblano to a medium bowl and cover the bowl. Allow the hot poblano to steam in the bowl for 10 minutes to loosen the skin. Once the poblano is cool enough to handle, remove and discard the skin, stem and seeds, then chop the pepper into small pieces.

Reduce the oven's temperature to 375°F (191°C). Lightly grease a large baking sheet. Slice the jalapeños lengthwise, leaving the stem attached. Set the jalapeños aside.

In a large bowl, combine the Neufchâtel cheese, poblano pepper, Cheddar cheese, Parmesan cheese, minced garlic, chili powder, smoked paprika, garlic powder, Himalayan pink salt, black pepper, red pepper flakes and cayenne pepper. Mix the ingredients together well.

In a medium bowl, combine the panko breadcrumbs and olive oil, lightly mixing the two together. Place the jalapeños on the prepared baking sheet, and then use a small spoon to fill each jalapeño with the cheese filling. Top each jalapeño popper evenly with the panko mixture. Bake the poppers for 12 to 15 minutes, until the jalapeños are tender and the filling is golden brown.

CREOLE-STYLE SALMON DEVILED EGGS

8 large brown eggs

⅓ cup (80 ml) crème fraîche

1 tbsp (9 g) minced garlic

½ cup (50 g) grated Parmesan cheese

1 tsp spicy brown mustard

2 tsp (10 g) dill pickle relish

1 tsp dried basil

1 tsp black pepper, divided

½ tsp smoked paprika

¾ tsp Himalayan pink salt, divided

¼ tsp cayenne pepper

1 lb (454 g) fresh skinless salmon fillets

½ tsp Creole seasoning

Classic deviled eggs get an upgrade! Crème fraîche replaces the usual mayonnaise to trim the extra fat and calories, while the tender salmon adds Creole-style oomph and the spicy brown mustard and dill relish turn this deviled egg recipe into one deliciously fresh and satisfying appetizer. They say good things come in small packages, and these bright and flavorful bites are proof.

In a large pot over high heat, boil the eggs for 20 minutes. Remove the pot from the heat, drain the water and allow the eggs to cool until they are safe to touch. Remove the shells. Slice the eggs in half lengthwise. Remove the yolks and place half of the yolks in a medium bowl; discard the remaining yolks or use them in another recipe. Add the crème fraîche, garlic, Parmesan cheese, brown mustard, relish, basil, ½ teaspoon of the black pepper, smoked paprika, ¼ teaspoon of the Himalayan pink salt and cayenne pepper. Stir the ingredients together to create a creamy filling. Set the filling aside.

Preheat the oven to 400°F (204°C).

Season the salmon fillets with the Creole seasoning, remaining ½ teaspoon of black pepper and remaining ½ teaspoon of Himalayan pink salt. Place the salmon fillets on a medium nonstick baking sheet and bake it for 5 minutes, until the salmon's internal temperature ranges between 125 and 135°F (52 and 57°C). Remove the salmon from the oven and cut the salmon into small chunks. Reserve a few pieces of salmon to use as a topping on the finished deviled eggs.

Add the salmon pieces to the bowl with the yolk mixture. Mix everything together until the filling is creamy. Fill each egg white half with the filling and top each deviled egg with a piece of the reserved salmon.

If you are not planning to serve the deviled eggs immediately, the egg whites, filling and salmon should be stored in the refrigerator for up to 2 days. Place the eggs whites in an airtight container, or place them on a medium baking sheet and wrap the baking sheet tightly in plastic wrap. Place the filling and salmon in separate airtight containers. When it's time to serve the deviled eggs, unwrap the egg whites and top them with the filling and salmon.

GUILT-FREE BAKED OKRA

I love okra! When I was younger, the only way I knew to make okra was by frying it. And while fried okra is one of my favorite foods, it's not exactly healthy. But what if you could get that same guilty-pleasure flavor without frying?

As it turns out, you can enjoy perfectly crispy okra by baking it in the oven. As a bonus, this okra recipe uses zero oil. Instead of using traditional breadcrumbs or cornmeal to coat the okra, I use panko breadcrumbs. These traditional Japanese breadcrumbs pack a lot of crunch and create lighter and crispier okra than conventional coatings. And if you're wondering how to rid yourself of okra's notorious slime, roasting not only enhances the flavor but it also reduces any sliminess.

With a new way to prepare okra, I've taken a classic southern appetizer and made it a little healthier. Make this panko-breaded okra just one time, and you may never fry okra again.

1 lb (454 g) fresh whole okra

1½ tsp (3 g) Himalayan pink salt, divided

¼ cup (32 g) arrowroot flour

1 cup (56 g) panko breadcrumbs

⅓ cup (33 g) grated Parmesan cheese

½ tsp garlic powder

1 tsp dried tarragon

1 tsp black pepper

2 large organic eggs

Preheat the oven to 375°F (191°C).

In a medium bowl, season the okra with 1 teaspoon of the Himalayan pink salt. Add the arrowroot flour and toss the okra to evenly coat it with the flour.

In another medium bowl, combine the panko breadcrumbs, Parmesan cheese, garlic powder, tarragon, black pepper and remaining ½ teaspoon of Himalayan pink salt. Mix the ingredients together thoroughly.

Crack the eggs into another medium bowl and whisk them together.

Shake the excess flour from the okra. Place it in the egg, then place it in the breadcrumb mixture, coating it evenly. Place the okra on a large nonstick baking sheet. Bake the okra for 15 to 20 minutes, until it is light golden brown and crispy.

CHEESY CAJUN RED SNAPPER SEAFOOD DIP

1 lb (454 g) fresh skinless red snapper fillets

1½ tsp (3 g) black pepper, divided

½ tsp Himalayan pink salt

1 tsp garlic powder

¼ cup (25 g) coarsely chopped celery

½ cup (75 g) coarsely chopped orange bell pepper

½ cup (25 g) coarsely chopped green onion

¼ cup (9 g) coarsely chopped fresh basil

½ cup (30 g) coarsely chopped fresh parsley

1 cup (232 g) low-fat cream cheese

1 cup (112 g) shredded Monterey Jack cheese, divided

¼ cup (60 ml) light mayonnaise

1 cup (100 g) grated Parmesan cheese

¼ cup (28 g) shredded Gouda cheese

1 tsp bottled lemon juice

1 tsp Creole seasoning

½ tsp ground thyme

This creamy fish dip is a household favorite and will be perfect for your next gathering, large or small.

Being a Louisiana native, I grew up eating all types of seafood. My father used to come home with plenty of shellfish. However, because my diet has changed over the years, I'm always looking for creative ways to incorporate fish in place of shellfish—even in recipes where you would traditionally find other ingredients. With this easy swap, you lower the cholesterol and sodium.

Using red snapper in this dish allows me to enjoy an appetizer I grew up with and enjoyed for so many years. Plus, if you have shellfish allergies, this dip is especially for you. This recipe still delivers on those seafood and Cajun vibes without compromising on flavor.

Preheat the oven to 400°F (204°C).

Season the red snapper fillets evenly with 1 teaspoon of the black pepper, Himalayan pink salt and garlic powder. In a 12-inch (30-cm) skillet over medium heat, cook the fillets for 1 to 2 minutes on each side, until their internal temperature reaches 145°F (63°C) and the flesh flakes easily. Cut the cooked red snapper into small chunks. Set the fish aside.

In a food processor, combine the celery, bell pepper and green onion. Pulse 2 to 3 times, until the ingredients are finely chopped. Add the basil and parsley, and process the ingredients for a few seconds, until the herbs are finely chopped. Set this mixture aside.

In a large bowl, combine the red snapper, cream cheese, ½ cup (56 g) of Monterey Jack cheese, mayonnaise, Parmesan cheese, Gouda cheese, lemon juice, Creole seasoning, thyme, remaining ½ teaspoon of black pepper and celery-pepper-onion mixture. Mix the ingredients together until they are well combined.

Transfer the dip to a 3-quart (2.9-L) baking dish and top the dip with the remaining ½ cup (56 g) of Monterey Jack cheese. Bake the dip for 15 minutes, until the cheese is bubbling and melted and the dip is hot throughout.

BAKED SALMON CROQUETTES WITH RÉMOULADE SAUCE

SALMON CROQUETTES

½ cup (51 g) coarsely chopped celery

½ cup (18 g) coarsely chopped fresh basil

1 lb (454 g) fresh skinless salmon fillets

1 cup (100 g) grated Parmesan cheese, divided

2 tsp (4 g) Creole seasoning

1 tsp black pepper

1 tsp dried oregano

¼ tsp garlic powder

½ tsp smoked paprika

1 large egg, beaten

½ cup (28 g) panko breadcrumbs

RÉMOULADE SAUCE

½ cup (120 ml) light mayonnaise

2 tbsp (30 g) dill pickle relish

½ tsp fresh lemon juice

¼ tsp Creole seasoning

¼ tsp garlic powder

¼ tsp smoked paprika

1 tsp hot sauce

¼ tsp white pepper

½ tsp horseradish sauce

¼ tsp Dijon mustard

Moist, tender chunks of fresh salmon combined with Creole seasonings and Parmesan, and dusted with panko breadcrumbs create a tasty bite. When it came to seafood, my grandmothers and mother fried pretty much everything by default. And croquettes were a quick and easy way for us to enjoy more of the same.

But my salmon croquettes are the opposite, and I'm officially going against the norm. These mini patties use fresh, nutrient-rich ingredients. This is an easy recipe loaded with chopped celery, fresh basil and lots of seasonings. Baked to a perfect golden brown, these delicacies can be enjoyed as appetizers or a main dish with a green salad or roasted veggies. Although excellent alone, they are upgraded when enjoyed with a side of my quick and tangy rémoulade sauce, which gives them a complementary creaminess.

To make the salmon croquettes, combine the celery and basil in a food processor. Process the celery and basil until they are finely chopped. Transfer the mixture to a large bowl.

Cut the salmon into small chunks. Add the salmon, ½ cup (50 g) of the Parmesan cheese, Creole seasoning, black pepper, oregano, garlic powder, smoked paprika and egg to the celery-basil mixture. Mix the ingredients together well, cover the bowl and refrigerate the mixture for 30 minutes.

Preheat the oven to 400°F (204°C). Lightly grease a large nonstick baking sheet.

In a medium bowl, combine the panko breadcrumbs and remaining ½ cup (50 g) of Parmesan cheese. Form the salmon mixture into small patties. Coat each salmon patty in the breadcrumb mixture.

Place the salmon patties on the prepared baking sheet, and then bake them for 12 to 15 minutes, until the croquettes are lightly browned and their internal temperature ranges between 125 and 135°F (52 and 57°C).

To make the rémoulade sauce, combine the mayonnaise, relish, lemon juice, Creole seasoning, garlic powder, smoked paprika, hot sauce, white pepper, horseradish sauce and Dijon mustard in a small bowl. Whisk the ingredients together until the rémoulade sauce is smooth.

Serve the salmon croquettes with the rémoulade sauce on the side.

COBB SALAD WITH HOMEMADE HONEY MUSTARD VINAIGRETTE

COBB SALAD

4 cups (960 ml) water

4 large eggs

1 lb (454 g) boneless, skinless chicken breasts

2 tsp (4 g) Creole seasoning

1 tsp dried oregano

1 tsp black pepper

1 tsp paprika

¼ tsp Himalayan pink salt

1 tbsp (15 ml) olive oil

12 oz (336 g) beef bacon

1–2 cups (149–298 g) cherry tomatoes

2 medium avocados

5 cups (235 g) romaine lettuce mix

I'll be honest. I remember the days when I would take a healthy salad and add so much dressing that you couldn't even tell it was salad anymore! Now though, I am making my dressing from scratch. It is truly the best way to enjoy salad and control the sugar, fat, sodium and calories you consume.

With this recipe, I make one of my favorite salads, the Cobb salad, and dress it with my homemade honey mustard vinaigrette. The salad boasts pan-seared chicken breast, romaine lettuce, cherry tomatoes, fresh avocados and hard-boiled eggs. The slightly sweet and tangy vinaigrette uses honey as a natural sweetener, vibrant white balsamic vinegar, tangy Dijon mustard, fresh lemon juice and zest and a slew of seasonings.

Whether you toss the dressing with all the ingredients, lightly drizzle it on the salad before serving or dip your ingredients in the dressing on the side, you'll be eating a guiltless salad that is fresh and better for you.

To make the Cobb salad, place the water in a medium pot over high heat and bring the water to a boil. Add the eggs and boil them for 20 minutes. Remove the eggs from the water and allow them to cool until they are safe to handle. Remove the shells. Slice the eggs in rounds, leaving the yolk intact. Transfer the eggs to a medium bowl and place the bowl in the refrigerator until you are ready to assemble the salad.

While the eggs are boiling, cut the chicken breasts into medium-sized cubes. Season the chicken evenly with the Creole seasoning, oregano, black pepper, paprika and Himalayan pink salt. Heat a 12-inch (30-cm) skillet over medium-high heat, then add the olive oil. Add the chicken and cook it for 5 to 7 minutes, until its juices run clear and the meat is completely opaque throughout. Set the chicken aside.

Preheat the oven to 400°F (204°C). Line a large baking sheet with parchment paper.

(continued)

HONEY MUSTARD VINAIGRETTE

¼ cup (60 ml) white balsamic vinegar

2 tbsp (30 ml) Dijon mustard

¼ cup (60 ml) raw unfiltered honey

1 tbsp (15 ml) olive oil

1 tsp lemon zest

1 tsp fresh lemon juice

½ tsp Creole seasoning

½ tsp black pepper

¼ tsp Himalayan pink salt

¼ tsp cayenne pepper

¼ tsp ground mustard

¼ tsp ground turmeric

COBB SALAD WITH HOMEMADE HONEY MUSTARD VINAIGRETTE (CONT.)

Place the beef bacon on the prepared baking sheet and bake it for 12 to 15 minutes, until the bacon is crispy and some of the fat has rendered. Remove the bacon from the oven and let it cool until it is safe to handle. Break it into medium-sized pieces. Set the bacon aside.

To make the honey mustard vinaigrette, combine the white balsamic vinegar, Dijon mustard, honey, olive oil, lemon zest, lemon juice, Creole seasoning, black pepper, Himalayan pink salt, cayenne pepper, ground mustard and turmeric in a small bowl. Whisk the ingredients together, and then transfer the dressing to the refrigerator until you are ready to serve the salad.

To finish preparing the Cobb salad, slice the cherry tomatoes in half. Peel the avocados, remove the pits and then thickly slice the avocados. Place the romaine mix in a large bowl, then top the lettuce with the avocados, eggs, cherry tomatoes, bacon and chicken. Drizzle the honey mustard vinaigrette over the salad and serve it immediately.

HONEY, LEMON AND PARMESAN BAKED CHICKEN WINGS

CHICKEN WINGS

3 lb (1.4 kg) chicken wings

1 tsp paprika

1½ tsp (3 g) black pepper, divided

1 tsp dried oregano

1 tsp Himalayan pink salt, divided

¾ tsp garlic powder, divided

¼ tsp ground cumin

¼ tsp ground thyme

½ cup plus 1 tbsp (135 ml) olive oil, divided

2 tsp (4 g) lemon zest

¼ cup (60 ml) fresh lemon juice

⅓ cup (80 ml) raw unfiltered honey

1 sprig fresh rosemary

1 leaf fresh sage

1 tsp dried basil

½ cup (50 g) grated Parmesan cheese

Three surefire ways to upgrade your wings: Season them to perfection, toss them in a honey-lemon glaze and serve them with homemade lemon-Parmesan aioli. One surefire way to make them healthier: Bake them! Baked wings are crispy, delicious and use a fraction of the oil required to deep-fry them. Made with fresh ingredients like lemon zest, natural honey, rosemary and sage, the herby glaze is so flavorful you won't care that the wings aren't fried. These game-day snacks are baked in the oven until the skin is perfectly golden and crispy—without using unhealthy oils or coating them in refined flour.

These wings are a great example of how I love to layer flavors. The wings start savory and then move to an herb coating that combines bright citrus, sweet honey and sharp Parmesan. I then boost those flavors with a mouthwatering aioli that reintroduces the Parmesan and lemon. Not only is this recipe delicious, but chicken wings will be the life of the party!

To make the chicken wings, preheat the oven to 400°F (204°C). Lightly grease a large nonstick baking sheet.

Cut each chicken wing at the joints to separate the drums and flats. Discard the wing tips. Place the wings in a large bowl, then season the chicken with the paprika, 1 teaspoon of the black pepper, oregano, ½ teaspoon of the Himalayan pink salt, ½ teaspoon of the garlic powder, cumin and thyme. Mix the wings together with the seasonings, then add 1 tablespoon (15 ml) of the olive oil and toss the wings to coat them in the oil. Place the chicken on the prepared baking sheet. Bake the chicken for 20 minutes, then flip the chicken wings over and bake them for 20 minutes, until their internal temperature reaches 165°F (74°C). For crispier wings, move the baking sheet to a higher rack after flipping the chicken wings.

Meanwhile, in a 2-quart (1.9-L) saucepan, combine the remaining ½ cup (120 ml) of olive oil, lemon zest, lemon juice, honey, rosemary, sage, basil, remaining ½ teaspoon of black pepper, remaining ½ teaspoon of Himalayan pink salt and remaining ¼ teaspoon of garlic powder. Cook the glaze over low heat for 8 to 10 minutes, until the glaze has thickened. Remove the glaze from the heat and remove the herb stems.

(continued)

LEMON-PARMESAN AIOLI

½ cup (120 ml) light mayonnaise

1 tbsp (9 g) minced garlic

3 tbsp (45 ml) fresh lemon juice

1 tsp lemon zest

3 tbsp (45 ml) olive oil

½ cup (50 g) grated Parmesan cheese

2 tbsp (30 ml) pure maple syrup

½ tsp dried oregano

½ tsp garlic powder

¼ tsp ground nutmeg

¼ tsp ground turmeric

½ tsp Himalayan pink salt

½ tsp black pepper

HONEY, LEMON AND PARMESAN BAKED CHICKEN WINGS (CONT.)

Transfer the baked chicken wings to a large bowl. Add the glaze and toss the wings to coat them with the glaze. Add the Parmesan cheese and toss the wings again to coat them with the cheese.

To make the lemon–Parmesan aioli, combine the mayonnaise, minced garlic, lemon juice, lemon zest, olive oil, Parmesan cheese, maple syrup, oregano, garlic powder, nutmeg, turmeric, Himalayan pink salt and black pepper in a medium bowl. Whisk the ingredients until the aioli is smooth.

Serve the chicken wings with the aioli on the side.

GARLIC AND PARMESAN STUFFED MUSHROOMS

2 lb (908 g) whole cremini mushrooms

½ cup (30 g) coarsely chopped fresh parsley

2 tbsp (30 ml) olive oil

1 tbsp (9 g) minced garlic

1 cup (224 g) Neufchâtel cheese

½ cup (50 g) grated Parmesan cheese

1 cup (112 g) shredded Gouda cheese, divided

½ cup (28 g) panko breadcrumbs, divided

2 tsp (4 g) dried basil

1 tsp black pepper

1 tsp smoked paprika

½ tsp ground thyme

½ tsp Himalayan pink salt

I've never met a mushroom I didn't like, but of all the different varieties, cremini mushrooms are at the top of my list. And when you stuff them, the love I have for mushrooms only deepens. Simply stated, stuffed mushrooms are awesome appetizers perfect for an anytime snack or when it's time to entertain.

Neufchâtel cheese, Gouda cheese, Parmesan cheese, garlic and various herbs and seasonings add to the deep umami flavor of the mushrooms. Once assembled, these stuffed mushrooms are baked to golden-brown perfection. This simple one-bite appetizer will turn anyone into a mushroom lover. Anyone.

Preheat the oven to 400°F (204°C). Lightly grease a large nonstick baking sheet.

Wash the mushrooms. Remove the stems and gills, reserving the stems and discarding the gills. Place the mushroom stems and parsley in a food processor and process them until they are finely chopped.

Heat a 12-inch (30-cm) skillet over medium heat. Add the olive oil, garlic and mushroom-parsley mixture. Cook the mixture for 5 minutes, stirring it occasionally, until the mushrooms are tender and lightly browned. Set the mushroom mixture aside.

In a medium bowl, combine the Neufchâtel cheese, Parmesan cheese, ½ cup (56 g) of the Gouda cheese, ¼ cup (14 g) of the panko breadcrumbs, mushroom mixture, basil, black pepper, smoked paprika, thyme and Himalayan pink salt. Mix the ingredients together well to create the filling.

Place the mushrooms on the prepared baking sheet, then stuff each mushroom with at least 1 tablespoon (15 g) of the filling. Top the stuffed mushrooms with the remaining ½ cup (56 g) of Gouda cheese and ¼ cup (14 g) of panko breadcrumbs. Bake the stuffed mushrooms for 15 to 20 minutes, until the mushrooms are lightly browned and the filling is golden brown.

CALLING ALL SIDES—
WITH FEWER CALORIES

The holidays feel like a giant food festival. It's when family and friends come together to enjoy feasts fit for kings and queens. Although turkey may have taken its place at the center of the table, everyone in my family was way more excited about the side dishes. With so many options to choose from, the strategy was to figure out how I could add them all to my plate. Which ultimately meant I had seconds, and that trip was made solely for the sides.

In this chapter, we are calling all sides to the table. These sides will showcase the ways we can enjoy sides without the guilt. Popular and must-have sides like Southern Potato Salad (page 112) are made using skin-on red potatoes to increase the nutritional value and add more texture. Cornbread is usually made with a lot of butter, which means a high number of calories and a high fat content; however, my Old-Fashioned Skillet Cornbread (page 115) comes fully loaded with goodies and is far from the traditional version—in it, you'll find fresh corn, jalapeños and raw honey. Baked sweet potatoes are great, but you have something special when you transform them into a fluffy soufflé. The flavor and sweetness in my Sweet Potato Soufflé (page 130) comes from using only natural sweeteners.

Collard greens are a staple in the South, and you'll fall hard for my Southern Collard Greens with Turkey Drums (page 118). Since the dish features turkey, it eliminates the extra sodium that generally comes from using ham hocks. And you cannot say "South" without saying "red beans." Red beans and rice are typically made with ham hocks, and they are loaded with salt. You can get that same taste without the extra sodium by just incorporating the right spices, using a minimal amount of salt and swapping the pork for turkey. My Red Beans and Rice with Turkey Sausage (page 122) is a hybrid of Cajun and Caribbean flavors that will stand tall next to any main dish. And as a bonus, Shanna has provided a healthier version of her family's Southern Green Beans and Potatoes (page 126). The green beans are flavorful, the potatoes are tender and the combination is downright tasty.

We all know sides are essential components to any meal. The goal isn't to take anything away from any flavor but to find ways to make the appropriate substitutions that don't compromise taste. It's no secret that you can have a wide range of healthy and unhealthy options when it comes to sides, but let's focus on the healthier side.

SOUTHERN POTATO SALAD

4 cups (960 ml) low-sodium vegetable stock

2 lb (908 g) red potatoes

3 large eggs

¾ cup (180 ml) light mayonnaise

3 tbsp (45 g) dill pickle relish

½ cup (25 g) coarsely chopped green onion

1 tsp spicy brown mustard

1 tsp minced garlic

1 tsp black pepper

1 tsp Himalayan pink salt

1 tsp dried oregano

1 tsp paprika

½ tsp Creole seasoning

¼ tsp ground mustard

⅛ tsp celery salt

"So, who made the potato salad?" This is a very important question and one I've heard many, many times at cookouts and family gatherings. You see, we take our potato salad very seriously here in the South. And there are many ways to make potato salad, and most are pretty similar; each one has a little more of this ingredient and a little less of that one.

A classic southern potato salad is rich, creamy and tangy. It's sweetened using dill relish, it's prepared using both brown mustard and mayonnaise and let's not forget the must-have hard-boiled eggs.

Since old-fashioned southern potato salad is traditionally made with lots of mayonnaise, this healthier version uses less mayonnaise. And I rely on red potatoes, which contain fewer calories and carbs than russet potatoes. The light dressing coats the tender potatoes and hard-boiled eggs, creating a satisfying dish that is full of flavor and texture. While these tweaks to the classic preparation make this potato salad better for you, the final product does not lack in the flavor department—in fact, this potato salad is the perfect companion to my Baked Barbecue Chicken Thighs (page 33), so eat up!

In a large pot, combine the vegetable stock and 8 cups (1.9 L) of water. Bring the stock and water to a boil over high heat. Add the red potatoes and cook them for 20 minutes, or until they are tender.

Meanwhile, in a small pot over high heat, bring 2 cups (480 ml) of water to a boil. Add the eggs and boil them for 20 minutes.

Drain the water from both pots and allow the potatoes and eggs to cool for 10 minutes.

Once the eggs are cool enough to handle, remove the shells. Slice the eggs in half, then remove and discard the yolks. Cut the egg whites into large pieces and set them aside.

Cut the cooled red potatoes into large cubes, being careful not to remove the skins.

Transfer the egg whites and the potatoes to a large bowl. Set the bowl aside.

(continued)

SOUTHERN POTATO SALAD (CONT.)

In a small bowl, whisk together the mayonnaise, relish, green onion, brown mustard, garlic, black pepper, Himalayan pink salt, oregano, paprika, Creole seasoning, ground mustard and celery salt.

Pour the dressing over the eggs and potatoes, and then fold everything together thoroughly.

Serve the potato salad warm or chilled.

2 cups (244 g) stone-ground yellow cornmeal

1 tsp baking powder

1 tsp Himalayan pink salt

⅓ cup (43 g) arrowroot flour

3 large eggs

1 cup (240 ml) evaporated milk

⅓ cup (73 g) brown sugar

¼ cup (60 ml) raw unfiltered honey

3 tbsp (45 ml) olive oil, divided

½ cup (77 g) fresh corn kernels

½ tsp paprika

½ tsp garlic powder

3 tbsp (42 g) unsalted butter, melted

1 cup (113 g) shredded medium Cheddar cheese

1 tbsp (2 g) dried parsley

½ cup (45 g) finely chopped jalapeño

⅓ cup (77 g) mascarpone cheese, at room temperature

OLD-FASHIONED SKILLET CORNBREAD

Moist, buttery cornbread with slightly crispy golden edges and the perfect density and crumb—it's the cornbread you've been searching for, and the only way to get it is in a cast-iron skillet.

While technically you can make cornbread in any dish, if you're looking for southern skillet cornbread, you've come to the right place. This cornbread is crunchy on the outside and tender on the inside, just the way I like it.

Lightly and naturally sweetened with honey to minimize the use of refined sugars, this savory cornbread can almost pass as a meal in itself. Yellow cornmeal blended with two types of cheese, fresh corn and jalapeños will become the staple side of cookouts and family dinners. Cut this cornbread into wedges and serve it alongside your favorite barbecued meat. It also goes great with my Red Beans and Rice with Turkey Sausage (page 122), Pinto Beans with Turkey Necks (page 121) and Southern Collard Greens with Turkey Drums (page 118). This dish is so heavenly that your family and friends will eat every last crumb.

Preheat the oven to 400°F (204°C).

In a large bowl, whisk together the cornmeal, baking powder, Himalayan pink salt and arrowroot flour. Set the cornmeal mixture aside.

In a medium bowl, combine the eggs, evaporated milk, brown sugar and honey. Whisk the ingredients until they are smooth. Set the egg mixture aside.

Heat an 8-inch (20-cm) skillet over medium heat, then add 1 tablespoon (15 ml) of the olive oil. Add the corn and season it with the paprika and garlic powder. Cook the corn for 5 minutes, stirring it occasionally, until it is tender and heated through. Remove the corn from the heat.

(continued)

OLD-FASHIONED SKILLET CORNBREAD (CONT.)

Add the butter, Cheddar cheese, parsley, corn kernels, jalapeño and mascarpone cheese to the cornmeal mixture, then mix everything together well.

Heat a 12-inch (30-cm) cast-iron skillet over medium-high heat, then add the remaining 2 tablespoons (30 ml) of olive oil. Pour the cornmeal batter into the skillet. Cover the skillet with aluminum foil. Bake the cornbread for 15 minutes. Remove the cover and bake the cornbread for another 15 to 20 minutes, until a toothpick inserted into the center comes out clean. Allow the cornbread to cool in the skillet for 15 to 20 minutes before serving it.

SOUTHERN COLLARD GREENS WITH TURKEY DRUMS

2 lb (908 g) turkey legs

2 tsp (4 g) smoked paprika

2 tsp (4 g) Himalayan pink salt, divided

1 tsp black pepper

½ tsp garlic powder

2 tbsp (30 ml) olive oil

1 cup (160 g) coarsely chopped white onion

2 tbsp (18 g) minced garlic

4 cups (960 ml) low-sodium chicken stock

1 lb (454 g) collard greens, washed and stems removed

1 tbsp (15 ml) apple cider vinegar

1 tsp dried oregano

1 tsp white pepper

½ tsp Creole seasoning

¼ tsp ground ginger

¼ tsp cayenne pepper

¼ tsp red pepper flakes

During the holidays when I was growing up, my plate was never complete without collard greens. Served alongside my meat of choice, mac and cheese, yams and cornbread, collard greens made with turkey brought it all together. They are a quintessential side dish.

They say you can't rush perfection, and you don't want to rush this recipe. The best way to cook southern-style collard greens is low-and-slow, as simmering the greens will result in a rich and deep flavor profile. You want all those pot juices to develop slowly and infuse the tender greens with the robust flavors of turkey drums and chicken stock. Turkey legs not only add more flavor to the greens, but they are also lower in fat than other traditional ingredients like ham hocks.

The red pepper flakes and cayenne pepper give these collard greens some kick, but the spice is balanced by the slight sweetness of apple cider vinegar, which also helps cut the bitterness from the greens themselves.

Season the turkey legs evenly with the smoked paprika, 1 teaspoon of the Himalayan pink salt, black pepper and garlic powder.

Heat a 12-quart (11.5-L) stockpot over high heat, then add the olive oil. Sear the turkey legs for 2 to 3 minutes on each side, until they are lightly browned. Remove the turkey legs from the heat and set them aside. Reduce the heat to medium and add the onion to the stockpot. Cook the onion for 5 minutes, stirring it occasionally. Add the minced garlic and chicken stock. Bring the stock to a gentle boil, then add the turkey legs back to the stockpot. Reduce the heat to medium-low, cover the stockpot and cook the turkey legs for 1 hour.

Increase the heat to medium, then add the collard greens, apple cider vinegar, oregano, white pepper, Creole seasoning, ginger, cayenne pepper, red pepper flakes and remaining 1 teaspoon of Himalayan pink salt. Stir the ingredients together, cover the stockpot and cook the collard greens and turkey legs for 1 hour, until the collards are very tender.

Remove the turkey legs from the pot and place them on a large cutting board. Once the turkey legs are cool enough to handle, use a fork to shred the meat, removing it from the bones. Transfer the shredded meat back to the pot. Serve the collard greens and turkey immediately.

PINTO BEANS WITH TURKEY NECKS

1 lb (454 g) dried pinto beans

2 tbsp (30 ml) olive oil

1 cup (160 g) coarsely chopped white onion

½ cup (75 g) coarsely chopped green bell pepper

2 tbsp (2 g) coarsely chopped fresh cilantro

2 tbsp (18 g) minced garlic

3 tsp (6 g) Himalayan pink salt, divided

1 tsp ground allspice

1 tsp ground cumin

1 tsp white pepper

1 tsp ground thyme

¾ tsp garlic powder, divided

1½ tsp (3 g) smoked paprika, divided

1 dried bay leaf

4 cups (960 ml) low-sodium chicken stock

2 cups (480 ml) canned light coconut milk

2 lb (908 g) turkey necks

1 tsp chili powder

½ tsp celery salt

½ tsp black pepper

1 tbsp (8 g) cornstarch

1 tbsp (15 ml) water

1 tbsp (15 ml) hot sauce

There's something about a big pot of pinto beans and a wedge of cornbread that always reminds me of home. The creamy consistency of the pinto beans is what makes this a favorite. And because they're versatile, pinto beans can be served with just about anything—and they are just as perfect on their own. If you're looking to increase the nutrition of your meal even more, I recommend serving this dish with cooked brown rice.

In this recipe, I keep things traditional: Dried pinto beans are soaked then cooked over low heat. And to make them even healthier, I've removed the salted pork, bacon and ham, instead opting for seasoned turkey necks. And what you get in the end is a delicious bowl of tender, smoky beans cradled in a silky, velvety pot juice.

In a large bowl of cold water, soak the pinto beans for 8 hours. Drain the beans and set them aside.

Heat a 12-quart (11.5-L) stockpot over medium heat, then add the olive oil, onion and bell pepper. Cook the vegetables for 5 minutes, stirring them occasionally. Add the pinto beans, cilantro, minced garlic, 2½ teaspoons (5 g) of the Himalayan pink salt, allspice, cumin, white pepper, thyme, ½ teaspoon of the garlic powder, ½ teaspoon of the smoked paprika and bay leaf. Stir the ingredients together well. Pour the chicken stock and coconut milk into the stockpot and bring the mixture to a gentle boil.

Meanwhile, season the turkey necks with the chili powder, celery salt, black pepper, remaining ½ teaspoon of the Himalayan pink salt, remaining ¼ teaspoon of garlic powder and remaining 1 teaspoon of smoked paprika.

Add the seasoned turkey necks to the stockpot, cover the stockpot, reduce the heat to low and cook the beans and turkey necks for 2 hours.

In a small bowl, whisk together the cornstarch and water to create a slurry. Remove the stockpot from the heat and add the hot sauce and cornstarch slurry. Let the beans and turkey necks rest for 5 minutes before serving them, stirring the ingredients occasionally, or until the sauce thickens.

RED BEANS AND RICE WITH TURKEY SAUSAGE

1 lb (454 g) dried small red beans

2 tbsp (30 ml) olive oil

3 tbsp (27 g) minced garlic

½ cup (80 g) coarsely chopped red onion

¼ cup (25 g) coarsely chopped celery

½ cup (75 g) coarsely chopped green bell pepper

¼ cup (15 g) coarsely chopped fresh parsley

½ cup (25 g) coarsely chopped green onion

1 tbsp (6 g) smoked paprika

1 tsp ground allspice

2 tsp (2 g) ground thyme

1 tsp white pepper

1 tsp rubbed sage

1 tsp dried oregano

½ tsp ground cumin

1 tsp Himalayan pink salt

¼ tsp cayenne pepper

1 dried bay leaf

3½ cups (840 ml) low-sodium chicken broth

2 cups (480 ml) canned light coconut milk

1 lb (454 g) smoked turkey sausage with beef casing, thinly sliced

Cooked white or brown rice, as needed

I grew up eating red beans and rice on the regular. I was raised by two grandmothers who made this dish constantly, and even though they each had their own spin on the dish, it was delicious in either home. My red beans and rice recipe combines what I learned from both grandmothers, with a few tasty tweaks of my own.

For a dish so complex in flavor, the preparation and ingredients are super simple. Along with the common ingredients, there are a few surprises, like coconut milk and turkey sausage. The coconut milk brings a wonderful velvety texture to the broth. And instead of pork, I've used turkey sausage for a lighter dish.

The recipe perfectly captures the simplicity that defines southern homestyle cuisine. Smoky, spicy, hearty and undoubtedly comforting, this recipe is perfect for feeding a crowd. After spooning these tender, flavorful red beans over fluffy rice, pair it with my Old-Fashioned Skillet Cornbread (page 115) and Southern Collard Greens with Turkey Drums (page 118) for a taste of home.

In a large bowl of cold water, soak the red beans for 8 hours. Drain the beans and set them aside.

Heat a 12-quart (11.5-L) stockpot over medium heat, and then add the olive oil. Add the garlic, red onion, celery, bell pepper, parsley and green onion and cook the mixture for 7 minutes, stirring it occasionally. Add the smoked paprika, allspice, thyme, white pepper, sage, oregano, cumin, Himalayan pink salt and cayenne pepper and cook the mixture for an additional 3 minutes, stirring the ingredients to combine them.

Add the red beans, bay leaf, chicken broth and coconut milk. Bring the mixture to a boil. Reduce the heat to medium, cover the stockpot and cook the beans for 30 minutes. Add the sausage and cook for 1 to 1½ hours, until the beans reach your desired tenderness. Serve the red beans and sausage with the brown rice.

CREAMY MASHED POTATOES

3 lb (1.4 kg) Yukon gold potatoes, peeled and cut into large cubes

¼ cup (57 g) unsalted butter

⅓ cup (80 ml) light sour cream

1 cup (240 ml) canned light coconut milk

2 tbsp (6 g) coarsely chopped fresh chives

2 cups (226 g) shredded sharp white Cheddar

½ cup (50 g) grated Parmesan cheese

2 tsp (4 g) Himalayan pink salt

1 tsp garlic powder

1 tsp black pepper

½ tsp onion powder

¼ tsp ground cumin

¼ tsp ground turmeric

Even with a table full of side dishes, the most loved side in our home is always that bowl of creamy, buttery mashed potatoes. As a matter of fact, I grew up on a steady diet of them. There are few entrées that don't pair well with mashed potatoes. And with only a few ingredients, this dish shows up quite often.

The secret to this recipe is not a ton of salted butter. Nope. It's a blend of cheese and light sour cream. And choosing the right potato will make a massive difference in the final product. And my go-to is Yukon gold. Yukon gold potatoes are naturally creamy, buttery and velvety in texture. Everything comes together to create a delectable side dish— while the unsalted butter and cheese provide that rich, sharp flavor, the sour cream keeps the potatoes moist and creamy.

Knowing how to make homemade mashed potatoes is a must for every home cook, and this easy recipe will produce guilt-free, creamy and buttery mashed potatoes every time. So put down that box of instant potatoes, and let's do this!

Bring a large pot of water to a boil over high heat. Add the potatoes to the water and boil them for 25 minutes, or until they are tender. Remove the pot from the heat and drain the potatoes. Transfer the cooked potatoes back to the pot and mash them with a potato masher.

Add the butter, sour cream, coconut milk, chives, Cheddar cheese, Parmesan cheese, Himalayan pink salt, garlic powder, black pepper, onion powder, cumin and turmeric to the potatoes. Mix the ingredients together with a handheld mixer until the mashed potatoes are smooth.

SOUTHERN GREEN BEANS AND POTATOES

1 tbsp (15 ml) olive oil

2 tbsp (28 g) unsalted butter

3 tbsp (27 g) minced garlic

1 cup (160 g) coarsely chopped sweet yellow onion

1½ lb (681 g) fresh green beans, trimmed

1 lb (454 g) red potatoes, cut in half widthwise

1 tsp Creole seasoning

2 tsp (4 g) Himalayan pink salt

1 tsp black pepper

1½ cups (360 ml) low-sodium chicken broth

½ cup (120 ml) water

This is the way folks in the South make their green beans!

This classic southern vegetable side dish is far from being bland and boring. Well-seasoned red potatoes cook until they're tender, while the green beans remain firm yet delicate. And my intentional omission of smoked meat keeps things light with all the flavor intact. This is a southern side dish you'll make again and again.

Heat a 12-inch (30-cm) sauté pan over medium heat. Add the olive oil, butter, garlic and onion and sauté the garlic and onion for 2 minutes, stirring them occasionally.

Add the green beans, red potatoes, Creole seasoning, Himalayan pink salt and black pepper. Sauté the mixture for 5 minutes, stirring it occasionally. Add the chicken broth and water. Cover the sauté pan, reduce the heat to medium-low and cook the green beans and potatoes for 40 to 45 minutes, until the green beans and potatoes are tender. Let the green beans and potatoes cool for 15 minutes before serving them.

SUPER SIMPLE CAJUN CABBAGE

3 tbsp (45 ml) olive oil, divided

1 lb (454 g) smoked turkey sausage with beef casing, thinly sliced

1 large head green cabbage

1 tbsp (14 g) unsalted butter

1 cup (89 g) coarsely chopped leek

3 tbsp (27 g) minced garlic

2 cups (480 ml) low-sodium vegetable stock

1 tsp Creole seasoning

1 tsp black pepper

1 tsp Himalayan pink salt

1 tsp dried basil

½ tsp ground thyme

½ tsp garlic powder

½ tsp celery salt

½ tsp ground ginger

¼ tsp ground allspice

¼ tsp cayenne pepper

A delicious way to eat your greens is this super simple stewed cabbage. This is an adaptation of the classic cabbage dish I grew up on. It's tender, carries a little kick and doesn't include any pork or other salty protein—the perfect accompaniment to chicken or roasted cod or halibut.

Cooked cabbage is one of those dishes that shows up in various cuisines—such as Polish, German, Irish and American (especially in the South)—and it's straightforward, as vegetable dishes go. The tightly bound head of greenish leaves transforms into a luscious pot of tender, melt-in-your-mouth greens with a mild flavor, making it the perfect base for my blend of Cajun seasonings. Cabbage is a magical vegetable, and southern cooks know this magic well.

Heat a 10-inch (25-cm) skillet over medium-high heat, and then add 1 tablespoon (15 ml) of the olive oil. Add the turkey sausage and cook it for 5 minutes, until it is lightly browned. Transfer the sausage to a small bowl and set it aside.

Cut the cabbage head into quarters, then remove the stem from each piece. Chop each quarter into 1-inch (2.5-cm)-wide strips. Set the cabbage aside.

Heat a 10-quart (9.6-L) stockpot over medium heat. Add the butter, remaining 2 tablespoons (30 ml) of olive oil, leek and minced garlic and cook the mixture for 5 minutes, stirring it occasionally. Add the vegetable stock and increase the heat to high. Add the cabbage, turkey sausage, Creole seasoning, black pepper, Himalayan pink salt, basil, thyme, garlic powder, celery salt, ginger, allspice and cayenne pepper. Stir the ingredients to combine them well, and then cover the stockpot. Cook the cabbage for 25 minutes, stirring it occasionally, until it is tender. Allow the cabbage to cool for 10 minutes before serving it.

SWEET POTATO SOUFFLÉ

3 large sweet potatoes

3 large eggs

½ cup (120 ml) light agave nectar

2 tbsp (30 ml) raw unfiltered honey

1 tbsp (15 ml) pure vanilla extract

2 tbsp (16 g) all-purpose flour

3 tbsp (42 g) unsalted butter, melted

2 tbsp (30 ml) olive oil

1 tsp baking powder

1 tsp ground cinnamon

1 tsp ground nutmeg

¼ tsp ground turmeric

¼ tsp Himalayan pink salt

If I could eat sweet potatoes with every meal, I would. They're so versatile and play well in both savory and sweet recipes. This time, I'm giving you a little sweetness in the healthiest way possible. Sweet potatoes pureed until silky smooth, then baked until light and puffed? Yes, please.

Unlike a sweet potato casserole, this dish is extra creamy and slightly fluffy, and I omit the traditional marshmallow, crumble or streusel topping to keep those calories down—after all, that baked sweet potato puree needs nothing to elevate it. For the sweet factor, I pair raw honey with agave nectar to eliminate any refined sugars. This soufflé is elegant yet rich and is perfect for your next holiday spread or any weeknight meal.

Preheat the oven to 400°F (204°C). Lightly grease a medium nonstick baking sheet.

Poke holes in the sweet potatoes with a fork. Place the sweet potatoes on the prepared baking sheet and bake them for 55 to 60 minutes, until they are tender. Remove the sweet potatoes from the oven and allow them to cool until they are safe to handle.

Reduce the oven's temperature to 350°F (177°C).

Peel the sweet potatoes, and then transfer them to a large bowl. Mash them using a potato masher until they are smooth. Add the eggs, agave nectar, honey, vanilla, flour, butter, olive oil, baking powder, cinnamon, nutmeg, turmeric and Himalayan pink salt. Mix the ingredients together with a handheld mixer until they are smooth and fluffy. Pour the sweet potato mixture into a 3-quart (2.9-L) baking dish. Bake the soufflé for 45 minutes, until it is firm in the center and lightly browned on top. Allow the soufflé to cool slightly before serving it.

SOUTHERN CREAMED CORN

2 tbsp (30 ml) olive oil

1 tbsp (14 g) unsalted butter

2 tbsp (16 g) arrowroot flour

3 tbsp (27 g) minced garlic

½ cup (80 g) finely chopped red onion

4 cups (616 g) fresh corn kernels

1 tsp black pepper

½ tsp Himalayan pink salt

½ tsp garlic powder

½ tsp smoked paprika

¼ tsp ground cumin

1 cup (240 ml) canned light coconut milk

½ cup (120 ml) low-fat 2% evaporated milk

⅓ cup (80 ml) raw unfiltered honey

1 cup (100 ml) grated Parmesan cheese

If you grew up in the South, you enjoyed fresh homemade creamed corn at some point. But if this is your first time, you're in for a treat. Made with freshly shucked sweet corn, this dish is creamy, a little sweet and oh so good. This is one dish where fresh ingredients can make or break it— it is best when made with peak-of-summer corn.

To make this version healthier, I swap the heavy cream for evaporated milk, coconut milk and Parmesan cheese. This combination still results in the rich flavor and silky consistency of the original that leaves everyone asking for seconds.

Heat a 12-inch (30-cm) sauté pan over medium heat. Add the olive oil, butter, arrowroot flour and minced garlic. Stir to combine the ingredients. Add the red onion and cook the mixture for 5 minutes, stirring it occasionally, until the onion is translucent. Add the corn, black pepper, Himalayan pink salt, garlic powder, smoked paprika and cumin. Cook the corn mixture for 5 minutes, stirring it occasionally. Add the coconut milk, evaporated milk and honey and cook the corn for 10 minutes. Remove the corn from the heat and fold in the Parmesan cheese. Allow the creamed corn to cool for 10 minutes before serving it.

A HEALTHIER WAY
TO RISE AND SHINE

Although sweet cereals and packages of oatmeal doused with tons of sugar and milk were the norm during my younger years, there was nothing quite like the smell of meat, eggs and grits in the morning. Pan-seared hot dogs, sausage or bacon with a side of buttered grits and eggs would set you on your way. Breakfast set the foundation for what would be a passionate culinary journey. When I was younger, the purpose of pulling together a hot breakfast for my family was to recreate those nostalgic feelings of waking the house with those familiar aromas.

From trying to light a gas stove using matches and a piece of paper to preparing a stack of pancakes from scratch, I've had an enjoyable culinary ride. My creativity in the kitchen was fostered during some humbled periods of life. It wasn't uncommon for me to eat breakfast for lunch or dinner, too, and it was pretty much a way of life during my high school years. Grams would have powdered eggs, powdered milk and "government cheese" wrapped in a brown cardboard container identical to the one the butter came in. It was just how things were at times. The humility I learned during those years allowed me to appreciate everything. As time went on, my exploration in the kitchen opened the doors of creativity. This was when dishes like omelettes stuffed with cheese, mushrooms and spinach became my new normal.

Once I got my hands on a waffle maker, I had fun creating various types of waffles while learning the proper techniques to achieve the desired texture. Having access to more information,

cooking tools and gadgets and better ingredients means I'm like a kid in the candy store when I'm in the kitchen. I'm now recreating some of the breakfast recipes I enjoy—and making them better for you at the same time.

When it came time to decide which breakfast recipes to share in this book, I faced a challenge —I have many good ones to share, but Shanna and I were able narrow them down to a few greats. There is nothing like fresh muffins from the oven, and since Shanna is the baker of the house, she chimed in with her awesome recipe for Healthy Blueberry-Banana Muffins (page 143). They are super moist and buttery, without a single drop of butter in the recipe. Grits are one of my favorite breakfast dishes, so I couldn't give you a breakfast chapter without incorporating them. But I'm not sharing typical grits—rather, I wanted to introduce you to my Cheesy Grits with Sausage and Peppers (page 136), in which polenta cooks in low-sodium chicken stock, making the dish a certified home run.

You'll thoroughly enjoy the Asparagus, Mushroom and Herb Frittata (page 140). This crustless, pillowy egg and cheese dish has a very balanced flavor profile, with earthy notes from the truffle oil. And there's always a debate between pancakes and waffles, so the deciding vote went to the kids. They loved my Healthy Banana-Nut Waffles (page 144), and you will too. Doctors say breakfast is the most important meal of the day—I'm hoping to make some of those days healthier and more memorable.

CHEESY GRITS WITH SAUSAGE AND PEPPERS

3 cups (720 ml) low-sodium chicken stock

1 cup (240 ml) canned light coconut milk

1 cup (156 g) yellow corn polenta

1 cup (112 g) shredded Gouda cheese

¼ cup (25 g) grated Parmesan cheese

1 tbsp (14 g) unsalted butter

¼ tsp red pepper flakes

½ tsp garlic powder

1 tsp Himalayan pink salt

1 tsp black pepper

1 tsp dried oregano

1 tbsp (15 ml) olive oil

1 lb (454 g) turkey sausage with beef casing, thinly sliced

½ cup (65 g) thinly sliced red onion

½ cup (46 g) thinly sliced red bell pepper

½ cup (46 g) thinly sliced green bell pepper

Rich, cheesy polenta joins forces with sautéed sausage and peppers for a breakfast that's on the table in less than ten minutes. Perfect as your main course or as a side, this dish is simple yet flavorful. It's the perfectly savory way to start the day.

It wouldn't be southern food without some grits. And these grits are extra special. I use yellow corn polenta for the texture, and although it takes slightly longer to cook, it's worth it. These grits boast two types of cheese, chicken stock and coconut milk for a ton of flavor.

The turkey sausage is sliced at an angle and sautéed in a bit of unsalted butter, and then it's combined with onion and bell peppers. The au jus created from the juicy sausage and vegetables provides the needed moisture for this dish. Spoon your sausage and peppers straight from the skillet over the hot grits, and boom!

In a 3-quart (2.9-L) saucepan, combine the chicken stock and coconut milk. Bring the mixture to a boil over high heat. Add the polenta, reduce the heat to low and cook the polenta for 5 to 7 minutes, stirring it occasionally. Add the Gouda cheese, Parmesan cheese, butter, red pepper flakes, garlic powder, Himalayan pink salt, black pepper and oregano. Stir the polenta until the ingredients are incorporated and the polenta is smooth. Remove the pot from the heat.

Heat a 10-inch (25-cm) skillet over high heat, and then add the olive oil. Add the turkey sausage, onion, red bell peppers and green bell peppers. Cook the vegetables for 5 to 7 minutes, stirring them occasionally, until they are tender.

Serve the turkey sausage and peppers over the cheesy polenta.

SWEET POTATO HASH

Versatile, filling and loaded with tons of great ingredients and nutrients, sweet potato hash is a healthy, simple meal—it's also the perfect place to put a delicious sunny-side up egg. There's just something about a runny egg that takes breakfast up a notch, am I right?

For a healthier spin, I made a few adjustments to the classic southern hash. First, I swapped white potatoes with sweet potatoes, as sweet potatoes contain more antioxidants, including vitamins A and C. Second, I sub leaner grass-fed beef bacon for pork bacon. I also include some jalapeños and bell peppers for extra color and flavor. Finally, a dollop of homemade spicy avocado aioli adds a hint of spice to the dish, and the aioli's creaminess brings all the ingredients together.

SWEET POTATO HASH

1 large sweet potato, peeled

¼ tsp ground turmeric

¼ tsp ground cinnamon

¼ tsp ground allspice

½ tsp Himalayan pink salt

3 tbsp (45 ml) olive oil, divided

½ cup (45 g) coarsely chopped jalapeño

½ cup (75 g) coarsely chopped red bell pepper

½ cup (75 g) coarsely chopped green bell pepper

2 large brown eggs

1 medium avocado, peeled, pitted and coarsely chopped

12 oz (336 g) beef bacon, cooked and crumbled

SPICY AVOCADO AIOLI

½ cup (120 ml) light mayonnaise

1 small avocado, peeled, pitted and mashed

1 tbsp (15 ml) Sriracha sauce

2 tsp (10 ml) fresh lemon juice

¼ tsp black pepper

¼ tsp ground thyme

¼ tsp red pepper flakes

¼ tsp cayenne pepper

¼ tsp smoked paprika

¼ tsp Himalayan pink salt

1 tsp dried cilantro

To make the sweet potato hash, cut the sweet potato into small cubes, then transfer them to a large bowl. Season the sweet potatoes evenly with the turmeric, cinnamon, allspice and Himalayan pink salt. Pour 1 tablespoon (15 ml) of the olive oil over the sweet potatoes and toss the cubes until they are evenly coated.

Heat a 12-inch (30-cm) cast-iron skillet over medium heat, then add 1 tablespoon (15 ml) of the olive oil. Add the seasoned sweet potatoes. Cover the skillet and cook the sweet potatoes for 20 minutes, stirring them occasionally, until they are tender and lightly browned.

While the sweet potatoes are cooking, heat an 8-inch (20-cm) skillet over medium-high heat. Add the remaining 1 tablespoon (15 ml) of olive oil, and then add the jalapeño, red bell pepper and green bell pepper. Cook the peppers for 5 to 7 minutes, stirring them occasionally, until they are tender. Transfer the cooked peppers to the sweet potatoes. Fold everything together.

Create 2 holes in the sweet potato hash and gently crack the eggs into those spaces. Cover the skillet and cook the eggs and hash for 3 minutes, or until the egg whites have set. Remove the skillet from the heat.

To make the spicy avocado aioli, combine the mayonnaise, mashed avocado, Sriracha sauce, lemon juice, black pepper, thyme, red pepper flakes, cayenne pepper, smoked paprika, Himalayan pink salt and cilantro in a medium bowl. Mix the ingredients until the aioli is smooth.

To serve the hash, top it with the chopped avocado, beef bacon and spicy avocado aioli. Serve the hash directly from the cast-iron skillet.

ASPARAGUS, MUSHROOM AND HERB FRITTATA

Frittatas are one of my go-to recipes when I want a quick breakfast or weeknight dinner. Boasting fresh asparagus, savory mushrooms and a delicious combination of rosemary, sage and parsley, this one-skillet meal is the perfect combination of protein and vegetables. The frittata gets its creaminess from a luscious combination of light sour cream, coconut milk, Gouda cheese and Cheddar cheese. Gently cooked at a low temperature, this creamy egg frittata is heaven in a cast iron.

2 tbsp (30 ml) olive oil

1 lb (454 g) asparagus, coarsely chopped

1 cup (70 g) coarsely chopped cremini mushrooms

1 tbsp (15 ml) white truffle oil

1½ tsp (3 g) Himalayan pink salt, divided

8 large eggs

½ cup (120 ml) canned light coconut milk

3 tbsp (27 g) minced garlic

2 tsp (2 g) finely chopped fresh rosemary

1 tsp black pepper

1 tsp rubbed sage

½ tsp ground cumin

½ tsp garlic powder

½ tsp dried parsley

1 cup (112 g) shredded Gouda cheese

1 cup (113 g) shredded New York extra sharp Cheddar cheese

⅓ cup (80 ml) light sour cream

Preheat the oven to 350°F (177°C).

Heat a 12-inch (30-cm) cast-iron skillet over medium heat, and then add the olive oil, asparagus and mushrooms. Cook the vegetables for 10 minutes, stirring them occasionally, until they are tender. Transfer the asparagus and mushrooms to a medium bowl. Add the truffle oil and ½ teaspoon of the Himalayan salt, then toss the vegetables to coat them with the truffle oil.

In a large bowl, combine the eggs, coconut milk, minced garlic, rosemary, black pepper, sage, cumin, garlic powder, parsley and remaining 1 teaspoon of Himalayan salt. Whisk the ingredients until they are smooth. Add the Gouda cheese, Cheddar cheese, sour cream and asparagus-mushroom mixture to the egg mixture. Stir the ingredients to combine them well. Transfer the frittata mixture to the cast-iron skillet. Place the skillet in the oven and bake the frittata for 30 minutes, until the center of the frittata is firm and the edges are golden brown. Allow the frittata to cool for 10 minutes before serving it.

HEALTHY BLUEBERRY-BANANA MUFFINS

2 large ripe bananas, unpeeled

½ cup (120 ml) raw unfiltered honey

¾ cup (180 ml) light sour cream

1 tsp pure vanilla extract

¼ cup (60 ml) olive oil

2 large eggs, at room temperature

1½ cups (180 g) white whole-wheat flour

1 tsp baking soda

½ tsp baking powder

¼ tsp Himalayan pink salt

1½ cups (222 g) fresh blueberries

When a muffin smells and tastes like banana bread combined with blueberry muffins, what else could you ask for? These fluffy, moist blueberry muffins are easy to make, and they are healthier than your average blueberry muffins. Made with fiber- and nutrient-rich white whole-wheat flour and naturally sweetened with honey and bananas, not only are these muffins better for you but they also taste great. With a few easy swaps, you can enjoy the coffeehouse-style muffins without all the extra calories.

Preheat the oven to 400°F (204°C). Spray a large 6-well muffin pan with nonstick spray.

In a medium bowl, use a fork to mash the bananas. Set the bananas aside.

In a large bowl, whisk together the honey, sour cream, vanilla and olive oil. Add the mashed bananas. Whisk the ingredients to combine them. Slowly whisk in 1 egg at a time.

In another large bowl, combine the flour, baking soda, baking powder and Himalayan pink salt. Slowly pour the banana mixture into the flour mixture. Gently fold the two together with a spatula. Gently fold in the blueberries. Do not overmix the batter.

Divide the batter between the prepared muffin wells, filling each one to the top. Bake the muffins for 15 to 18 minutes, until a toothpick inserted into the center of a muffin comes out clean. Remove the muffin pan from the oven and place it on a wire rack. Allow the muffins to cool slightly before serving them.

HEALTHY BANANA-NUT WAFFLES

1 large ripe banana

1½ cups (180 g) whole-wheat flour

1 tsp lemon zest

1 tsp ground nutmeg

½ tsp ground cinnamon

¼ tsp ground turmeric

¼ tsp Himalayan pink salt

1 tsp baking powder

2 large egg yolks

1 tbsp (15 ml) pure vanilla extract

1 cup (240 ml) low-fat 2% evaporated milk

¼ cup (60 ml) raw unfiltered honey

⅓ cup (80 ml) melted coconut oil

2 large egg whites

¾ cup (75 g) walnuts, finely chopped

Pure maple syrup, sliced banana and walnut pieces, as needed

These waffles passed the ultimate test: When my kids asked for these waffles three weekends in a row, I knew I was on to something! I've always considered waffles an indulgent breakfast to be reserved for special occasions, but when they are as good for you as these are, you can make them every weekend if you wish.

Made with whole-wheat flour, ripe banana, honey, spices and coconut oil, these waffles are effortless to make. Plus, they're free from refined sugars. Enjoy these fluffy waffles topped with fresh fruit, a drizzle of honey and a few extra walnuts for a guilt-free breakfast.

Preheat the waffle maker according to the manufacturer's instructions.

In a medium bowl, mash the banana with a fork until it is smooth. Set the bowl aside.

In a large bowl, whisk together the flour, lemon zest, nutmeg, cinnamon, turmeric, Himalayan pink salt and baking powder. Set the flour mixture aside.

In a medium bowl, combine the egg yolks, vanilla, evaporated milk, mashed banana and honey. Mix the ingredients together with a handheld mixer. Add the melted coconut oil and mix until the ingredients are well combined.

Add the egg mixture to the flour mixture and mix the two together until the batter is smooth. Set the batter aside.

Place the egg whites in a medium bowl. Beat the egg whites with a handheld mixer for 4 to 5 minutes, until they stiffen and form peaks.

Fold the walnut pieces into waffle batter, then lightly fold in the egg whites.

Cook each waffle for 3 to 5 minutes in the waffle maker, or until the waffle reaches your desired crispiness. Serve the waffles hot with the maple syrup. Top with banana slices and walnuts.

THE GUILTLESS
SWEET TOOTH

Who didn't grow up with a sweet tooth? During my childhood, I was on a constant lookout for my next sugar rush. My wife, Shanna, laughs whenever I tell the stories of my sugar escapades.

I didn't do much baking growing up, but I was always around when the baking was going down. I had to ensure I had a seat at the table for the taste test, especially when my mother would make cakes and left my younger brother, sister and me to finish off the icing left in the mixing bowl. One of my mom's cakes in particular was the most memorable. She would create a cake with jelly bursting out from between the layers. You could tell she made each dessert with love, and you could taste that love in each bite.

My mother and grandmother set the bar high for desserts, so I was pleasantly surprised when my wife showcased her baking skills. Shanna claimed she was a baker when we met, and she made me a believer with her recipes. I now rely on her heavily when it comes to baking, so she took the lead on this chapter and knocked it out of the park. Not only can Shanna bake anything, but she can also create healthier desserts that can easily satisfy a person with a sweet tooth as large as mine. For this, I am grateful.

Every dessert in this chapter is different. A few are baked, a few are not, and the flavors up the ante from the traditional. For example, the Bourbon Apple Crisp à la Mode (page 157) gets its sweetness naturally from maple syrup rather than a ton of refined sugar. The Low-Fat Sweet Potato Cheesecake (page 153) is another winner Shanna created by combining a layer of cheese-cake with layers of sweet potato—it is off-the-charts good. And if you want something unique, try the Banana Crème Brûlée (page 158). It brings together all the things you love about banana cream pie and crème brûlée and meshes them together in a dessert that is better for you than either of those traditional desserts. These recipes are the one time you can enjoy dessert before dinner and feel okay about it.

SOUR CREAM POUND CAKE

1 cup (227 g) unsalted butter, softened, plus more as needed

1 cup (200 g) sugar

1 tbsp (15 ml) pure vanilla extract

6 large eggs

3 cups (375 g) all-purpose flour

1 tsp salt

½ tsp baking soda

1½ cups (360 g) light sour cream

Light whipped cream, fresh berries and powdered sugar (optional)

Old-fashioned pound cake reminds me of Sundays after church. If I wasn't the first in line to grab my to-go plate, I was a close second. The tender crumb and subtle sweetness of pound cake made Sunday my favorite day of the week.

This sour cream pound cake proves that a simple dessert can often be your best-kept secret. And even when you keep things simple, you don't need a ton of sugar or fat to make it unforgettable. Made with light sour cream and baked in a Bundt® pan, this cake is dense, buttery and moist—all the things you want a cake to be! My family loves this cake served with a low-fat whipped topping and fresh fruit.

Preheat the oven to 325°F (163°C). Grease a 10-cup (2.4-L) pan with the additional butter.

Place 1 cup (227 g) of the butter in a large bowl, and then beat it with a handheld mixer until it is smooth. Add the sugar and vanilla. Mix the ingredients for 1 to 2 minutes, until they are smooth and creamy. Add the eggs one at a time, mixing between each addition.

In another large bowl, lightly whisk together the flour, salt and baking soda. Slowly add the flour mixture to the butter and egg mixture. Do not overmix the batter. Fold in the sour cream.

Pour the cake batter into the prepared pan. Bake the cake for 75 minutes, until a toothpick inserted into the center comes out clean. Remove the cake from the oven, and allow it to cool for at least 20 minutes, or until it has completely cooled. Invert the cake pan to remove the cake, then serve it. Top with light whipped cream, fresh berries and powered sugar (if using).

HEALTHIER SOUTHERN PEACH COBBLER

You can't have a list of southern desserts and not include peach cobbler. It's just not right. But instead of using a canned fruit drowned in syrup, go with fresh or frozen peaches this time around! This healthier-for-you version uses maple syrup, cuts down on the sugar and incorporates must-have flavors like vanilla, cinnamon and nutmeg to create a healthy and delicious fruit-filled treat that will satisfy any dessert craving.

CRUST

1¼ cups (156 g) all-purpose flour, plus more as needed

1 tsp granulated sugar

½ tsp Himalayan pink salt

½ cup (114 g) cold unsalted butter

6 tbsp (90 ml) cold water

1 large egg, beaten

Pinch ground cinnamon

FILLING

5 cups (770 g) thickly sliced fresh or thawed frozen peaches

½ cup (120 ml) pure maple syrup

¼ cup (55 g) light brown sugar

1 tsp ground cinnamon

½ tsp bottled lemon juice

1 tsp pure vanilla extract

¼ tsp ground nutmeg

1 tsp cornstarch

1 tsp water

To make the crust, combine the flour, granulated sugar and Himalayan pink salt in a medium bowl. Cut the cold butter into small pieces. Add the butter to the flour mixture and, using a pastry cutter, incorporate the butter into the flour until crumbs appear. Slowly add the cold water to the flour and mix it into the flour using your hands or a spatula until the dough starts to form a ball.

Dust a work surface with additional flour. Transfer the dough ball to the prepared work surface and knead it 4 to 5 times, until it is smooth and elastic. Tightly cover the dough with plastic wrap and place it in the refrigerator to chill for 30 minutes.

Preheat the oven to 375°F (191°C). Lightly grease 2 (6½-inch [16-cm]) cast-iron skillets.

To make the filling, combine the peaches, maple syrup, brown sugar, cinnamon, lemon juice, vanilla and nutmeg in a large bowl. Stir the ingredients together well.

In a small bowl, combine the cornstarch and water to create a slurry. Add the slurry to the peaches. Mix everything together well and set the bowl of filling aside.

(continued)

HEALTHIER SOUTHERN PEACH COBBLER (CONT.)

Pour the peach mixture into the prepared cast-iron skillets. Set the skillets aside.

Dust a work surface with additional flour. Remove the dough from the refrigerator, unwrap it and place it on the prepared work surface. Using a rolling pin, roll out the dough until it is ¼ inch (6 mm) thick. Cut the dough into 2-inch (5-cm)-wide strips. Arrange the dough strips in a lattice pattern on top of the peach filling. Brush the dough with the beaten egg, and then sprinkle the dough with the cinnamon. Bake the cobblers for 30 minutes, until the crust is golden brown and the filling is bubbly. Allow the cobblers to cool on a wire rack for 30 minutes before serving them.

LOW-FAT SWEET POTATO CHEESECAKE

1 large sweet potato

1½ cups (348 g) low-fat cream cheese, at room temperature, divided

½ cup (110 g) granulated sugar, divided

1 tsp ground cinnamon

1 tsp ground nutmeg

1 tbsp plus 1 tsp (20 ml) pure vanilla extract

1 cup (60 g) low-fat whipped topping

12 graham crackers

1 tbsp (14 g) brown sugar

½ cup (114 g) unsalted butter, melted

Mint (optional)

We love an easy dessert, and when we can forgo the oven for the fridge, that makes it even better. When it comes to chilled desserts, all you need is a little time—once the dessert is set, the real party begins.

And what makes this treat even better is the addition of roasted sweet potato—roasting brings out the potato's natural flavor and sweetness, making it an extra special part of this dessert. The creamy and spiced root vegetable sits between a slightly sweet low-fat cheesecake layer and a buttery graham cracker crust for the main event.

Preheat the oven to 350°F (177°C). Lightly grease a small nonstick baking sheet. Line the bottom and sides of an 8 x 8–inch (20 x 20–cm) baking dish with parchment paper.

Using a fork, poke a few holes into the top of the sweet potato. Place the sweet potato on the prepared baking sheet and bake it for 1 hour, until it is tender. Allow the sweet potato to cool until it is safe to handle. Remove the skin from the sweet potato and transfer the flesh to a medium bowl. Mash the sweet potato using a potato masher. Add ½ cup (116 g) of the cream cheese, ¼ cup (55 g) of the granulated sugar, cinnamon, nutmeg and 1 teaspoon of the vanilla to the sweet potato. Use a handheld mixer to combine the ingredients until they are smooth. Set the sweet potato mixture aside.

In a large bowl, combine the remaining 1 cup (232 g) of cream cheese, remaining ¼ cup (55 g) of granulated sugar and remaining 1 tablespoon (15 ml) of vanilla. Using a handheld mixer, mix the ingredients until they are smooth. Add the whipped topping and fold the ingredients together. Set the cream cheese mixture aside.

(continued)

LOW-FAT SWEET POTATO CHEESECAKE (CONT.)

Place the graham crackers in a large ziplock bag and crush them into fine pieces with a rolling pin. Transfer the crushed graham crackers to a large bowl. Add the brown sugar and butter. Mix the ingredients together well.

Transfer the graham cracker mixture to the prepared baking dish, pressing the mixture evenly into the bottom of the dish. Pour the sweet potato mixture over the graham cracker crust and spread it out evenly. Carefully pour the cream cheese mixture over the sweet potato layer, spreading it out evenly.

Refrigerate the cheesecake for at least 8 hours before serving it. When you are ready to serve the cheesecake, lift it from the casserole dish using the parchment paper. Cut pieces of cheesecake with a cookie cutter, or slice the cheesecake into even squares. Add fresh mint as garnish (if using).

BOURBON APPLE CRISP À LA MODE

4 cups (500 g) peeled and finely chopped Honeycrisp apples

⅓ cup (80 ml) pure maple syrup

1¼ tsp (4 g) ground cinnamon, divided

½ tsp ground nutmeg

1 tbsp (15 ml) bourbon

1 tbsp (15 ml) apple juice

3 tbsp (42 g) brown sugar, divided

¾ cup plus 2 tbsp (198 g) unsalted butter, melted

2 tbsp (16 g) cornstarch

2 tbsp (30 ml) water

½ cup (63 g) all-purpose flour

½ cup (45 g) rolled oats

½ cup (63 g) pecans, coarsely chopped

¼ tsp Himalayan pink salt

Light vanilla ice cream, as needed

Fresh, tender, cinnamon-laced apples topped with generous crumbles of crust and ice cream is what desserts are all about. Sure, I enjoy all three—the apples, the crumbles and the ice cream—but they are hard to beat when they come together as a team.

The apples are peeled and chopped into the bite-sized pieces to ensure you get a little bit of everything in each bite. And because we want the apples to shine and not get lost in overpowering sweetness, they are tossed in delicious maple syrup and bourbon with a bit of brown sugar and some spices, which bring it all home. The pecans in the crispy oat crumble give this dessert some extra texture, and when the light ice cream melts and makes its way into the tiny nooks and crannies of the crisp, you better believe it's going to be good.

Preheat the oven to 350°F (177°C). Lightly grease as 12-inch (30-cm) baking dish.

In a large bowl, combine the apples, maple syrup, 1 teaspoon of the cinnamon, nutmeg, bourbon, apple juice, 1 tablespoon (14 g) of the brown sugar and 2 tablespoons (28 g) of the butter in a large bowl. Mix the ingredients together with a spatula. In a small bowl, combine the cornstarch and water to create a slurry. Add the slurry to the apple mixture and stir to combine everything. Set the apple filling aside.

In a large bowl, combine the flour, rolled oats, remaining 2 tablespoons (28 g) of brown sugar, pecans, remaining ¼ teaspoon of cinnamon, Himalayan pink salt and remaining ¾ cup (170 g) of butter. Mix the ingredients together with a spatula until a crumbly dough forms.

To assemble the crisp, pour the apple filling into the prepared baking dish. Sprinkle the crumbly dough on top of the apples. Bake the crisp for 40 to 45 minutes, until the apples are tender and the topping is golden brown. Remove the apple crisp from the oven and allow it to cool for 15 minutes.

Serve the apple crisp à la mode with the vanilla ice cream.

BANANA CRÈME BRÛLÉE

2 tbsp (28 g) unsalted butter, divided

2 large ripe bananas, thinly sliced

1 tbsp (14 g) light brown sugar

2 cups (480 ml) 2% milk

½ cup (120 ml) canned light coconut milk

½ cup plus 3 tbsp (142 g) granulated sugar, divided

½ tsp Himalayan pink salt

4 large egg yolks

¼ cup (32 g) cornstarch

1½ tsp (8 ml) pure vanilla extract

An incredible fusion of banana cream pie and crème brûlée, this dessert is all the things you love from both—served in individual ramekins for a perfectly sized treat.

It starts with a few slices of fresh banana and just gets better from there. The slightly rich banana and vanilla-flavored custard get a boost of creaminess from the coconut milk, which also complements this dessert with its sweet, nutty flavor. The finale comes by way of the flambéed layer of sugar, giving this dessert a hint of sweetness and bringing you one step closer to the fluffy surprise waiting underneath.

In a 10-inch (25-cm) sauté pan over medium heat, melt 1 tablespoon (14 g) of the butter. When the butter has melted, add the bananas and brown sugar, stirring to combine the ingredients. Cook the bananas for 5 minutes, stirring them occasionally, until the bananas are slightly caramelized. Remove the sauté pan from the heat and transfer the bananas to a small bowl. Mash the bananas with a fork until they are smooth. Divide the banana among 6 (5-ounce [150-ml]) ramekins.

In a 3-quart (2.9-L) saucepan, combine the milk, coconut milk, ½ cup (100 g) of the granulated sugar and Himalayan pink salt. Whisk the ingredients together, and then bring the mixture to a boil over medium-high heat, stirring it frequently. As soon as it begins to boil, reduce the heat to low. Transfer 1 cup (240 ml) of the milk mixture to a small bowl.

In a medium bowl, whisk together the egg yolks and cornstarch. Add the 1 cup (240 ml) of milk mixture to the egg mixture. Add this egg and milk mixture back to the saucepan. Stir the custard for 1 to 2 minutes, stirring it constantly, until it thickens. Remove the custard from the heat and add the vanilla and remaining 1 tablespoon (14 g) of butter. Stir the ingredients to combine them.

Pour the custard over the bananas in the ramekins. Allow the custard to cool for 15 minutes, and then cover the ramekins with plastic wrap. Refrigerate the ramekins for at least 4 hours.

Before serving the crème brûlée, sprinkle the remaining 3 tablespoons (42 g) of granulated sugar evenly over the custard in each ramekin. Caramelize the granulated sugar with a small kitchen torch.

ACKNOWLEDGMENTS

Writing this cookbook has been one of the most rewarding yet challenging experiences we've ever faced. Our goal was to bring people closer to understanding the importance of what we put in our bodies. And through each thoughtfully curated recipe, we hope to accomplish that goal. We are so grateful for the path the Lord has placed us on and the many people who played a significant role in this process. This book would not be possible without the tremendous amount of support we have received.

To Tamara Grasty and the Page Street Publishing team, thank you for believing in us enough to invest your time, resources and support in Dude That Cookz and making this project a reality.

To our fantastic photographer, Amy Scott, thank you so much for your incredible energy and great eye that brought every recipe we created to life. You made this process easy, especially on those long days of shooting. We are happy to call you a friend.

To our families that supported this culinary ride from the beginning, we want to truly thank you for all your support and encouragement as we stepped outside of our comfort zone. A special thank you to Sharon Tate for being our biggest cheerleader and encouraging us along the way. We appreciate you. Another special thank you to Erica Jones and Victor Jones; this is a win for all of us. You were witness to many of the stories we shared throughout this book.

To Eric's "Bourbon Brothers," you all are like family to me and have always shown me the utmost support. I appreciate you guys for being my taste testers. And to Rodney Williams, the group organizer, thank you for your honest feedback and advice as we created these recipes.

To Natalie Arceneaux and Marvin Martin, thank you for not only supporting us through this journey since the very beginning but also for becoming voluntary recipe testers, whom we didn't even have to ask. Thanks for always showing up. And Dr. Roberta Scott, thank you for being one of our biggest fans. We love you.

To our family who are no longer with us but had just as much of a role in getting us through this book as anyone else: Eric's mother, Beverly Jones; father, Eric D. Jones; grandfather Herman "Daddy Paul" Bynum; grandmother Pearl "Momma Pearl" Bynum; grandmother Helen "Grams" Dupree; and Shanna's father, Rodney Tate. The memories we shared brought this cookbook to life. Thank you all for everything you sacrificed. We miss you.

To our beautiful children, Ireon Jones and Jeriah Jones, you are the reason we remain focused and work hard. You two are our toughest food critics, and we want to thank you for pushing us to make sure everything will be great for everyone else.

And last but not least, to the readers of Dude That Cookz, thank you from the bottom of our hearts. Your encouragement and support gave us the confidence and motivation we needed to accept such a blessing. This book would not be happening if it wasn't for you all.

—Matthew 6:31–33

ABOUT THE AUTHORS

Eric and Shanna Jones are the husband-and-wife team behind Dude That Cookz, a popular food and recipe blog. While both share their creative space when developing recipes, they work independently as well, honing their individual passions.

Eric, a Louisiana native and self-taught home cook, shares southern and homestyle recipes using simple, clean, approachable ingredients. Born and raised in Houston, Texas, Shanna focuses on her love for baking and food photography.

Eric and Shanna's work has appeared online and offline in *Essence* magazine, BuzzFeed, Taste of Home, SELF, Food52, *Southern Cast Iron* magazine, *Women's Health* and *The Pioneer Woman*. Shanna and Eric currently live in Houston. *Healthier Southern Cooking* is their first book.

INDEX